HOW TO: SPEAK WITH CONFIDENCE IN PUBLIC

Edie Lush is a journalist and communications coach. As a coach, she has helped clients shine in big speeches, promotion panels, interviews, pitches, literary festivals, board meetings, media appearances and TED talks. She is Executive Editor of Hub Culture and regularly interviews CEOs, entrepreneurs and politicians, and chairs events around the world. As a journalist, she has worked for Bloomberg TV, the BBC, *The Spectator*, *Prospect*, *The Week* and *Spectator Business* magazines. She has been a political analyst for a hedge fund and a speechwriter for the Secretary General of the Organization of American States, and is a graduate of UCLA and Yale. She lives in London and works in the UK and US.

Charlotte McDougall is a communication and leadership coach. She works with people to develop leadership skills, win new business, increase personal impact and build strong client relationships. Charlotte is also an actress and comedy writer who has performed with Cate Blanchett, Miranda Hart and Ronnie Corbett. She wrote and starred in the Radio 4 comedy sketch show *The Bearded Ladies*, and her recent appearances include *Downton Abbey*, *We're Doomed*, *The Inbetweeners*, *Misfits*, *The Paradise* and *Charlotte Grey*.

how to: ACADEMY launched in September 2013. Since then it has organized over 400 talks and seminars on Business, Lifestyle, and Science & Technology, which have been attended by 40,000 people. The aim of the series is to anticipate the needs of the reader by providing clarity, precision and know-how in an increasingly complex world.

Edie Lush with Charlotte McDougall

HOW TO: SPEAK WITH CONFIDENCE IN PUBLIC

bluebird
books for life

First published 2016 by Bluebird
an imprint of Pan Macmillan
20 New Wharf Road, London N1 9RR
Associated companies throughout the world
www.panmacmillan.com

ISBN 978-1-5098-1453-4

9 8 7 6 5 4 3 2 1

A CIP catalogue record for this book is available from the British Library.

Printed and bound by CPI Group (UK) Ltd, Croydon, CR0 4YY

Visit **www.panmacmillan.com** to read more about all our books
and to buy them. You will also find features, author interviews and
news of any author events, and you can sign up for e-newsletters
so that you're always first to hear about our new releases.

Contents

1: Introduction 1

2: Dynamic energy 6

3: Telling the story 41

4: The science behind this stuff 65

5: Preparing for an interview 73

6: Case study: the job interview 89

7: The Big Speech 94

8: The body is wired for images 108

9: Case study: the Big Speech 114

10: How to start – and end – strong 120

11: Case study: pitching for business 129

12: Conclusion 140

Authors' Note 143

Acknowledgements 145

Index 147

1:

INTRODUCTION

Jerry Seinfeld once joked that most of us would rather attend a funeral in the casket than give the eulogy. Many of us would agree. A 2013 poll in the UK had glossophobia – the fear of speaking in public – as the second largest fear (after losing a family member). Fear of being buried alive – or just dying – came third and fourth, respectively.* Why does the thought of standing up in front of a group make our knees knock and our voice tremble?

Think about all the times you've drifted off in a meeting,

---

* 'Speaking in public is worse than death for most', *The Times*, 30 October 2013.

or in a class. All the times you've listened to a speech and it has just failed to land. Most of us are guilty of reaching for our mobiles to send a message during a presentation, and of getting caught there for several minutes before turning back to the speaker. This is despite knowing how it feels to be on the reverse side of the podium. As speakers, we have all noticed people gazing out of the window or getting sucked into the black hole of their phone screens while our own mouths have been open, our carefully composed words pouring out.

At the heart of this book is the idea that *good communication is about building connections*. This is true whether you're a head girl giving a talk at school, a political candidate speaking to a crowded room, a CEO giving a conference speech, a graduate going for a first interview, a scientist giving a TED talk or anyone, anywhere, having a meeting.

We all know what it is like when we have connected with someone, even just one-on-one. We can see the person we're talking to smiling and nodding as we speak. We feel visible, memorable and in control of the impact we make.

But what can happen when we feel in the spotlight, or when we need to deliver, is that the confident, comfortable and engaging person our friends recognize can drain away to leave a drier, less effective version of ourselves. We might disappear into a rabbit hole of detail. We might use thirty words when three would do. We might forget the point we are trying to make. We might just appear worried and nervous. This can have devastating effects on us. At best, our message may fail to land, leaving our audience unmoved. At worst, the audience may make negative judgements that impact on whether they buy into us as a speaker and a person.

We live in a world where everyone is short of time and attention.

Yet, despite this, we all know those people who manage to command attention. People who speak with gravitas and authority. People who get listened to. People who charm, entertain or persuade with their words. People who get hired.

How can you be compelling *and get buy-in* to both yourself and your ideas? To do so, it is vital that you are aware of your personal brand and style and in control of how others perceive you.

What are the skills that enable you to develop solid relationships? What are the techniques that build rapport and win confidence and trust? How can you sell your ideas and products while letting your personality and warmth come through?

This book will help you build your presence and profile, and explore techniques to help you present yourself, your personality and your message in a confident, personable and compelling way – wherever you are, and whomever you are talking to.

We'll look at the obvious but often overlooked qualities of effective communication and impact. By exploring the concepts of dynamic energy (to increase presence) and telling a story (to bring to life what you say and make it concise, accessible and memorable), we'll work on putting you in control of your impact and content so that you come across as engaging, *personable* and authoritative. This is the foundation for real self-awareness and self-assurance.

We believe that – just as everyone can learn to play a better game of tennis, or a musical instrument – everyone can learn to speak in public.

This book tells you how.

What you'll learn from the following pages:

- A heightened awareness of what effective and engaging communication looks and sounds like.

- Practical techniques to take away and immediately put into practice, which will help you come across with more confidence and authority.

- A practical methodology to help you prepare and structure your content and bring it to life.

- How to control nerves.

- How to make your communication resonate with your audience.

The book is divided into chapters that address many of the public speaking opportunities in which you'll find yourself in life, like job interviews, big speeches and business pitches. Feel free to dip in and out – but don't skip Chapters 2 and 3, on 'dynamic energy' and 'telling the story'. These concepts are at the heart of the book. The case studies come from real work we've done with real clients. There's some science – not too hard core – in Chapters 4 and 8, which explains why our theories work and will show you why – if you make these techniques your own – you'll be unstoppable. Or at least memorable and interesting, whenever you open your mouth.

2:

DYNAMIC ENERGY

This chapter is about what it takes to look and sound comfortable and confident, regardless of how you're feeling inside.

Why is it that when one person starts to speak, we sit up and listen – then, when another person speaks, we switch off and zone out? More often than not, we do the latter. Whether we are at school, at university or at work, we rarely find speakers who are truly engaging. Think about the teachers and lecturers you have known. I have copious memories of time in the classroom moving imperceptibly slowly, of listening to a dull monotone and watching an expressionless face. Consequently I doodled, wrote a shopping list, or – even worse – nodded off. But it was a subject I was passionately interested in! I had signed up to study it! So how could they make it so dull?

In our business lives we are communicating all the time – on the phone, on conference calls, at internal meetings, pitching to a new client, speaking to the entire company, being interviewed for a new job. How often do we walk away from a meeting or presentation thinking 'I really enjoyed that,' or 'Wow, that was interesting'? Not very often. In fact, we usually walk away thinking 'That went on a bit,' or 'I thought he was never going to finish.' This strikes me as a waste of everyone's time. No one wants to be described as dull. No one wants to be described as 'a bit of a bore'.

So, what is effective and engaging communication all about?

In my fifteen years as a communication coach working with businesses, teachers and graduates all over the world, what I come across, again and again, is that the written word and the spoken word get muddled up. For me, the two are radically different.

Dr Albert Mehrabian is Emeritus Professor of Psychology at UCLA, and is best known for his publications on the relative importance of verbal and non-verbal communications. In his studies, Mehrabian concludes* that there are basically three elements to any face-to-face communication:

- words
- tone of voice
- non-verbal behaviour (e.g. facial expression).

For Mehrabian, the non-verbal elements are particularly important for communicating feelings and attitude. If the words disagree with the tone of voice and non-verbal behaviour, people tend to believe in the latter.

Mehrabian is often quoted as saying that the meaning of a message is communicated by:

- your words: 7 per cent
- your tone of voice: 38 per cent
- your body language: 55 per cent.

There are recognized limitations to Mehrabian's experiments and results. There has been debate and disagreement

---

* Albert Mehrabian, *Silent Messages*, 1971.

about his findings. However, there can be no doubt that *how* we speak and how we *appear* when we speak can have a significant impact on our ability to land messages and engage listeners.

For example, if a CEO of a business addresses his or her employees with the claim, 'I feel hugely confident about the success of this business,' but delivers what he says with an anxious expression or in a dull monotone, then he or she is giving a mixed message. It is incongruent. How a speaker delivers their message, and how they come across when they are delivering their message, have a huge influence on how we, the audience, feel about them. Do we like them, do we feel confident about them, do we want to work with them? Are we going to be influenced by what they say?

Similarly, anthropologist Ray Birdwhistell* looked at non-verbal communication in his study of what he calls 'kinesics'. He estimated that the average person actually speaks words for a total of ten or eleven minutes a day, and the average sentence takes about 2.5 seconds. Birdwhistell also estimated that we can make and recognize around 250,000 facial expressions.

His findings were similar to those of Mehrabian:

- The verbal part of a face-to-face conversation is less than 35 per cent.

- Over 65 per cent of communication is non-verbal.

Allen and Barbara Pease† recorded thousands of sales

---

* Ray Birdwhistell, *Kinesics and Context: Essays on Body Motion Communication*, 1970.
† Allen and Barbara Pease, *The Definitive Book of Body Language: The Secret Meaning Behind People's Gestures*, 2008.

interviews and negotiations in the 1970s and 1980s. They showed that in business meetings body language accounts for between 60 and 80 per cent of the impact made around a negotiating table. They also found that 60–80 per cent of a negotiator's initial opinion about a new person in the room was formed in less than four minutes.

So we don't have long to grab people's attention. Body language is important.

How can we make our message land?

Good news: there is an ingredient that guarantees our message will land every time.

I would much rather be described as a 'warm radiator' than a 'cold pipe'. We have all experienced meeting a 'cold pipe' in a social situation or at work. They are dry. They are dull. They are to be avoided. What cold pipes lack in their communication style is *dynamic energy*. This is the magic ingredient.

I love this idea of dynamic energy. It allows us to be interesting, engaging and, importantly, to have personality. Cold pipes have none of these qualities. In fact, they tend to sap the energy from other people.

Thinking about all the different communication situations you find yourself in at work, what most affects your energy levels? The answer is *how you feel*. Tiredness makes the most obvious impact. Perhaps you have a new baby who is not sleeping through the night? Perhaps you have been out late the night before? Perhaps you haven't been kick-started by your regular morning espresso? There might be other factors. How do you feel about the meeting? Perhaps you are bored by the content. Do you think this meeting is a waste of time? Are you nervous? Is your boss in the room, and is he or she always critical of your performance? Perhaps you are nervous because you have an opportunity to pitch to a new client and you don't want to mess it up. Or perhaps you are nervous because you haven't had enough time to prepare?

All of these factors affect your energy levels. All of these factors affect your ability to be effective.

Let's imagine you are giving one of your clients a project update. Ideally, you would have liked more time to prepare. But you have done some homework and feel pretty confident about the meeting ahead. You begin with the client update and get off to a good start. The energy in the room is positive. Suddenly the most senior stakeholder interrupts by throwing you a challenging and unexpected question. You are surprised. You fumble for an answer, and eventually offer a long-winded and repetitive response. You can feel your energy levels drop. However, you take a deep breath and get back on track. It starts to go well again. The energy picks up. But then you catch sight of one of your clients tapping away on their phone. Clearly they have not registered your most recent and very interesting point. Why are they finding their phone more interesting than you? Why are they being so rude? Unsurprisingly, your energy levels take a nose-dive.

Your tankful of energy turns out to have a leak. As we've seen, it is other people who affect our energy levels. It's the client who asks tough questions. It's the partner looking out of the window. It's the person in the audience looking at you with a completely blank expression. In fact, it turns out that the most stressful audience is one that gives nothing back. Professor Marianne LaFrance of Yale University calls this 'standing in social quicksand'. I've heard these kinds of audiences (or clients, or meeting participants) called 'mood-Hoovers'. I personally like to call them 'energy vampires', because they just suck the confidence and energy right out of you.

Let's have a think about what is happening to your listeners during this meeting.

If you aren't in control of your energy, and the energy level is dropping, what happens to the listener? What are they thinking and feeling?

The first thing that happens is that they switch off and zone out. We all do this *all* the time. Think back to sitting in a lecture hall with ineffective teachers or university lecturers. Suddenly we're miles away, thinking about what we want for lunch or what to buy for our daughter's birthday, wondering about our next meeting.

The second thing that happens is more dangerous. When we are not being engaged, we often start to make judgements and assumptions about the speaker. 'She looks rather uncomfortable.' 'Why is he taking such a long time to make this minor point?' 'She's on the longlist for promotion this year, but I'm not sure she's ready.' Unfortunately our profile, image and brand are being assessed every time we communicate – in a meeting, on a call or during a presentation.

We have to be in control of what we project.

Our energy levels can be reactive and erratic during a meeting. They can be inconsistent and unpredictable, too. Yet it is clearly not helpful for us to be perceived as inconsistent or erratic. So, in order to come across as consistent and in control, we need to change our energy levels. We need to take them up. We need more power.

Over the years my clients have come up with wonderful synonyms for this concept of extra energy or power. 'Oomph', 'gusto', 'pizzazz' and 'dynamic' are some of my favourites. Having 'oomph' allows us to lead and steer the energy levels in the meeting room. Human beings mirror one another: we mirror each other as energy vampires, and we mirror each other when we are using dynamic energy.

I asked Olivier Oullier, Professor of Behavioural and Brain Sciences at Aix-Marseille University in France, why this is. He told me about his work on what he calls 'social coordination dynamics'.* He and his colleagues placed pairs of people in front of one another and asked them to make a series of movements. It was up to them which movements they chose. First they performed their movements with their eyes closed. When they could not see each other, their movements were not influenced by each other. But when Professor Oullier asked his pairs to open their eyes while performing their movements, their actions started to mirror each other. In Oullier's scientific world, this is called 'spontaneous interpersonal synchronization'. We can settle on 'mirroring'.

What is intriguing about Oullier's work is that the behaviour of each individual remained influenced by the social encounter even after the information exchange had been removed. It became what he calls a kind of social memory. When asked to perform their action again, there were 'remnants and echoes' of the other person's movements. This suggests that if you are dynamic, or full of energy in your speech, your audience can become more energetic and actively engaged in what you are saying.

We've all experienced the moment when someone yawns, and we yawn back (in fact, we only have to see a picture of someone yawning to trigger the yawn impulse in ourselves). Equally, when someone smiles at us, we tend to

---

* Olivier Oullier et al., 'Social coordination dynamics: Measuring human bonding', 2007.

smile back. This is because our brain mirrors what others do, and encourages us to do the same.

Taking responsibility and consciously upping our energy levels means that our listeners start, unconsciously, to increase their own energy. The negative cycle begins to turn positive.

How high do our energy levels have to be?

The short answer to this is: higher than you think. In order to be engaging and compelling, we have to switch something on. The good news is that this is something we are used to doing. Think about the last time you had a party: in host/hostess mode, you instinctively have more energy and vibrancy than anyone else in the room. Think about a first date: you are hyper-aware of how irresistible, attractive and witty you want to appear. In such situations, your energy levels shoot up without your knowing it. But at work, when you are speaking in public or during an important meeting, you have to learn how to *consciously* switch on your energy.

What does dynamic energy look and sound like?

I have had some wonderful responses to this in the training room:

- alive
- pleased to be there
- comfortable
- relaxed
- animated
- enjoying ourselves
- confident
- effortless

- authoritative
- composed
- powerful

- calm
- charismatic
- present

How can we be perceived when we don't have dynamic energy?

- nervous
- bored
- bland
- uncomfortable
- unhappy
- tense
- awkward

- self-conscious
- dull
- fidgety
- low status
- wanting to get it over with
- wooden
- unmemorable

Low dynamic energy makes you feel less powerful

In 1822, Charles Darwin identified that expansiveness among animals equals power. Chimpanzees pick up sticks and hold them out to make themselves look bigger. Cobras physically expand. Cats make their hair puff out in order to increase their size. A great deal of work has been done around how humans do the same when they feel powerful. Amy Cuddy's research on the effect of body posture on our minds is fascinating in this regard.[*]

Think of gymnasts when they finish a routine. They lift

_____

[*] Amy Cuddy, *Presence: Bringing Your Boldest Self to Your Biggest Challenges*, 2015.

their chin and hold up their arms. When a sprinter is first to cross the finishing line, she throws her hands in the air. What is fascinating is that even congenitally blind people do this – it is a totally innate response to winning, or to feeling power. When a sports team wins, fans on the winning side of the stadium throw their arms into the air as a sign of victory. They feel powerful, confident and assertive. Equally, when we feel powerless, we physically shrink. We tilt our heads in submissiveness. We cross our legs when we stand. We try to make ourselves look smaller.

Cuddy's work is around how we can reverse these occurrences. We can change how we feel by changing the way we sit and stand. Cuddy has looked at how our posture is always communicating information to our minds. Testosterone is the chemical released by the brain when we feel assertive, confident, risk-tolerant and competitive. Cortisol makes us feel stressed, anxious, insecure, fearful, defensive and risk-avoidant. When we expand, the testosterone increases and the cortisol decreases. If we hold positions of higher power – what Cuddy calls 'power poses' – we can actually start to change the chemicals our brain releases. We can decrease the cortisol levels and increase the testosterone levels. Clinical psychologists have discovered that making people sit up straight leads to them feeling more optimistic. Children who sit more upright when they take exams are found to write more creatively.

This work has implications for us as speakers. The way we stand or sit can affect how we feel. So let's look at how to give ourselves the best chance of feeling, as well as looking, confident and composed.

What are the ingredients that make up physical energy?

Everyone can learn techniques for increasing their energy and animation levels.

First, let's look at physical energy.

Posture: sitting down

BIG NO: It is tempting to tuck ourselves in to the meeting table and rest our elbows/hands either on the table or the arms of the chair. The table can provide a nice comfort blanket for us. We can hide behind it. This is dangerous because it means our 'core' collapses (think Pilates) and we appear slumped, saggy and physically smaller than we are. At its worst, we appear physically timid or apologetic. This posture can increase your cortisol levels. You are not doing your mind any favours by sitting this way.

You might reach for a pen as another kind of comfort blanket. Danger: it can be distracting for others to watch you twiddle with your pen.

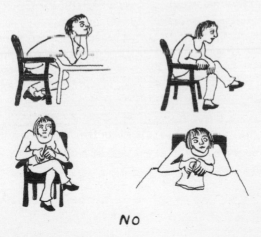

NO

BIG YES: Take your chair away from the table and sit up tall. Put the pen down! Make sure your knees aren't tucked in to the table, uncross your legs and plant both feet firmly on the ground in front of you. Imagine there is a string pulling up to the sky from the crown of your head. At first it feels odd, it feels forced. But this is about owning your space and managing your presence. We have to literally 'be present' at the table.

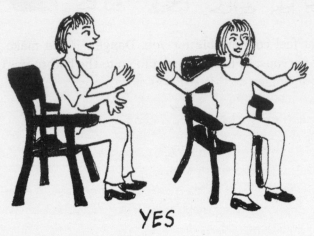

YES

Posture: standing up

As an audience we immediately make judgements and assumptions based on the visual cues we are being given. With no table to hide behind, standing can make us feel exposed and vulnerable.

BIG NO: Standing with weight on one leg – you might imagine you look relaxed. Danger: it can appear over-casual or awkward.

Standing with one leg crossed in front of the other – this

might feel comfortable for you. Danger: it can make you look nervous, or like you need to go to the bathroom. I see a lot of women do this. It seems as if they are trying to make themselves smaller – as if they don't deserve to be present. They are afraid of getting found out.

Head on one side – you might imagine that you look empathetic, full of listening and understanding. Danger: this pose can appear apologetic or cause your status to drop. It can also come across as condescending.

Standing behind a lectern – this might feel safe and comfortable. Danger: it's a barrier between you and the audience you are trying to connect with. For me, it says, 'I don't like public speaking, I don't like being looked at, I am not feeling confident here.' As an audience member, it also suggests that I am about to be 'transmitted at' by someone rather than 'talked with'. For bigger events when you need to speak into a microphone, always insist on a lapel mic with a battery pack so that you can walk around.

What do I do with my hands?

Ah, the big question. I have been asked this countless times. Isn't it peculiar that when we are in the spotlight or under pressure, suddenly our hands start to feel like strange bananas at the ends of our arms and we don't know where to put them or what to do with them? These are some of the things that we tend to do to compensate:

Hands behind our back – danger: we look like policemen or nightclub bouncers.

Hands in pockets – danger: over-casual, 'I don't give a damn.'

Hands twiddling and fidgeting, e.g. with a pen or a wedding ring – danger: I'm feeling nervous and agitated up here.

Hands on hips – danger: can appear aggressive or confrontational. We look like a cowboy. Amy Cuddy would point out that this is a power pose, which is true. However, it looks weird on stage, especially when held for extended periods of time.

BIG YES: Make sure you are positioned *directly facing* the audience. Stand with your feet positioned at the width of your hips, and your weight evenly distributed. Check that your chest is open rather than collapsed. Imagine there is a string attached to the crown of your head pulling you up to the sky. Now you are starting to own your space. You are starting to look tall, open and comfortable. Your cortisol levels will drop, and your testosterone will rise.

Hands. Get them moving! Use them to illustrate and orchestrate everything you say. Avoid 'T-Rex arms' – your hands moving, but your elbows pinched to the side.

If your hands are clamped to your sides, your shoulders will become tense, which can make you seem uncomfortable and self-conscious. Instead, imagine big balloons under your armpits to help fill and own the space to the side of you. Keep your hands moving!

This is what we do in real life. When you are having dinner with friends and family and someone is telling a story, watch them. When we are feeling unselfconscious and relaxed, we are animated and moving the whole time. WE ARE USING OUR HANDS. We exude positive energy.

So, to help us appear relaxed and comfortable at times when we are feeling unrelaxed and uncomfortable, what we have to do is to recreate *consciously* what we do *unconsciously* in more relaxed situations.

Vocal energy

What about vocal energy? These are some of the things that can happen to our voice when we are feeling nervous or under pressure:

Too quiet – our listeners strain to hear. Danger: it's hard work for them, and they switch off.

Monotone – our voice becomes trapped on one or two notes. Danger: we sound bored or disengaged. Our listeners also become bored.

Swallowing words – a common habit is to swallow the last few words at the end of a sentence. This is also called the 'dying fall'. Danger: the end of our sentence is inaudible and the meaning is lost. Our listeners zone out.

Rushing – one sentence collides with the next, with no break in between. Or we stop using the sentence structure completely. It's a word trifle, or stream of consciousness. Danger: it's hard work for our listeners, and they can't keep up.

Running out of breath or sounding breathless. Danger: our voice can sound nervous or lightweight.

Ending the sentence sounding like a question ('upspeak') – I often hear this from younger people. Danger: it decreases your status, and sounds like you aren't sure of yourself.

What are the ingredients that make up vocal energy?

The human voice is a wonderful natural instrument. Think of the dynamism, colour and power in the voices of children. It's impossible to accuse a crying baby or a toddler having a tantrum of having low vocal energy! Sadly, on the journey from childhood to adulthood we somehow disconnect from this vocal ease and expressiveness. Most of us, with the exception of actors, opera singers, barristers and clergy, have forgotten how to use our voices. So what are the techniques to help us reconnect and engage our audiences?

Double the volume

I have a theory that at some point in our lives, we make a subconscious choice about how much noise we are going to make and how much space we are going to take up. This is where we feel comfortable. It's linked to how confident we feel about ourselves. But in a meeting, on a conference call or when we are giving a presentation, the default setting you have chosen needs to be adjusted. I'm not suggesting that you use so much volume that you might be described as 'loud'. However, in order for your voice to have any chance of sounding interesting and animated, you have to turn up your personal amp.

So, *use double the volume that you feel comfortable with*. When I do vocal energy exercises with clients, I often ask them to double the volume. I meet resistance. 'I just can't do that.' 'It's not me.' 'I feel like I'm shouting.' But when we watch the exercise back on camera they are astonished at what they hear. 'My voice hasn't got any louder at all despite the fact that it felt like I was shrieking my head off.' 'I think I need to be louder still.' A tiny adjustment from the default setting of your voice feels ENORMOUS. So if you're trying to double the volume and it feels like you're deafening everyone, it's probably about right.

Emphasis

Use emphasis all the time. This probably sounds bonkers. In real life, we emphasize words when they are important, when we are emotionally connected to them. With our business messages, this can be difficult to do. The result is that our voices start to lack colour. Instead of reds and blues and yellows and golds, we communicate in a vocal grey. It's dull and difficult to engage with.

By contrast, it's fascinating to eavesdrop on people who are communicating with animals – there is so much variety, intonation and colour in our voices when we talk to Crumpet the dog or Monty the cat. We never tell someone that we love them in a dull monotone. They wouldn't believe us.

In the training room, one of my exercises is to encourage a client to emphasize *every. single. word*. They will often say that they feel implausible, idiotic or clownish and firmly state that they would NEVER do this in a real presentation or meeting. But – just as with the volume exercise mentioned above – we then watch it back on camera, and at this point the client is astonished. They will say, 'It sounds normal.' 'It sounds like I'm really interested in this topic.' 'It's so much more interesting to listen to.' 'I think I need to use more emphasis.'

Why is emphasis important?

It slows you down. It is easy to gabble and rush when we are nervous. The danger here is that it can sound like we want to get it over and done with. It can sound uncomfortable and out of control. Emphasis is a brilliant technique to help slow you down.

In a written document, the reader can read and then re-read if necessary to understand the message clearly. When it comes to the spoken word, the listener has only one chance. The words come and go in a flash. Using emphasis halves the pace of your voice and doubles the impact of what you are saying.

It helps you connect with your content. In real life, we don't say, 'Iloveyourlittledoghe'sadorable.' We say 'I LOVE your dog. He's ADORABLE.' This is because we are emotional creatures. We feel. In business, it is easy to disengage with our feelings and sound robotic. Emphasis helps us start to become emotionally connected again. It gives the impression of commitment to what we are saying – it reassures listeners that what we have to say is important.

I have often been asked, 'But what if I emphasize the wrong word or syllable?' There is nothing to worry about here. We are sophisticated, sentient beings. Our instincts and intelligence are such that we NEVER put emPHAsis on the wrong syllABle.

Microphones

It is easy to assume, when we are using a microphone at a conference or speakerphone on a conference call, that the microphone will do all the work so that there is no need for us to project vocally. Unfortunately this is not the case. The microphone amplifies only what it is given. If you are communicating with low vocal energy, in a flat, grey monotone, the microphone will amplify that low vocal energy. It might be a bit louder, but your audience will not engage.

Emphasis gives our words weight and value. By extension, it gives *us* weight and value.

Pause

Here are two rules for pausing:

- Pause three times more often than feels comfortable.
- Pause for three times longer than feels comfortable.

We all know someone who 'never draws breath' or 'won't let you get a word in edgeways'. Such people can leave us feeling frustrated, infuriated and exhausted. We soon stop listening to someone who is in 'transmit' mode. It's hard work to stay engaged, and so we start 'pretending' to listen when, actually, we are miles away.

Pausing is a crucial ingredient of vocal impact. For many of my clients it is the most important ingredient – and the hardest to put into practice.

Imagine trying to read a newspaper or magazine article with no capital letters, no paragraphs, no full stops, no commas – no punctuation of any kind.

atusc'sinstituteofcreativetechnologiesinla,thefutureis hereandit'svirtualafterwritingaboutgooglecardboard anditspredecessoradevicemadebytheuniversityof southerncalifornia'sinstituteofcreativetechnologieslast week,irealizedihadalayoverofseveralhoursinlosangeles. seeingastheinstituteliesonlya15minutedrivefromthe airport,icouldn'tresistavisit.whatifoundstrollingaround theinstitute'smixedrealityresearchlabwasaviewofthe futurei'dseenbeforeonlyinbooks.inoneroomidonnedaset ofvirtualrealitygogglesandenteredamilitarytraining exerciseinafghanistanwhereiwandereddownadusty street,inandoutofbuildings(appropriatelyaccessorised withkilimrugs)lookingforacacheofhiddenweapons. whenitookthegogglesoffifoundiwasinaroomwithblack curtainsandaconcretefloorratherthanadustybackstreet oflashkargah.whatwasfascinatingwasthattheareai'd exploredwasmuchlargerthantheroomiwasin.iwasableto dothisbecauseofatechniquecalled'changeblindness' inventedbyevansuma,aresearchassistantprofessoratict andtheuscdepartmentofcomputerscience.asientereda virtualroom,thelocationofthedoori'dwalkedthrough switchedfromonewalltoanother.thismeantthatwheni turnedaroundtowalkoutofthedoor,iwaswalkingina differentdirection.thisideaof'stretchingspace'has profoundimplicationsitmeansthatyouaren'tlimitedtothe physicalspaceyouhavetoexplorevirtualworlds.

This article[*] I wrote about visiting a virtual reality studio in Los Angeles is almost impossible to read. We don't bother. Likewise with verbal communication. A monologue excludes the listener because if we are 'transmitted at', we feel kept out rather than let in. Pausing is verbal punctuation.

Benefits of pausing

For the speaker – time to think. As speakers, we need time to gather our thoughts and choose the correct word or phrase. When we are relaxed with our friends and family, we always give ourselves time to think. However, when we are in the spotlight or under pressure, we deny ourselves this time, and feel that we have to keep talking.

---

* Edie Lush, 'Virtual doctors: easier to talk to than the real thing', The Week.co.uk, 14 July 2014.

But why multitask when you don't have to? Thinking and talking at the same time is stressful and pressured. It results in neither action being effective and makes us come across as rambling, repetitive and unclear. So my advice is to *pause, think, talk*.

For the listener – time to digest. Imagine a dance class where you are learning tricky new steps, but the dance instructor keeps moving on to the next step before you've mastered the one before.

If listeners are not given time to digest and absorb points, they struggle. They are at the back of the class playing catch-up. It's hard work, and the danger is that our listeners stop listening. We don't want our audience to disengage. So don't drown them in a torrent of words. Communicate to them in small, bite-sized, easily digestible chunks.

Anticipation. A pause can put us on the edge of our seats. What is he or she going to say next?

Gives the listener 'nodding time'. It is very frustrating to be communicated at, in a monologue. It is alienating. Regular pausing can turn a piece of communication that feels like a monologue into something that feels like a dialogue. *Relationships are built in the pause.* If we see our listeners nodding in the silence, it is a sure sign they are with us. Equally, if you see someone looking a little confused, there's the opportunity to check in with them. We all know the moment when a presentation can 'feel like a conversation'. Pausing helps do that.

Gives us gravitas. Puppies have a tendency to yap. *Yap, yap, yap.* They yap because they are inexperienced, over-excited and fearful. Yapping is a sign that they are junior. Older, more experienced dogs tend not to yap. Rather, they bark when they have something important to communicate. They are experienced. They are senior. For me, someone who can sit comfortably in a pause, unflustered by silence, displays status, calm and seniority. They want to be perceived as authoritative.

We can read the written word again, but we hear the spoken word only once. Harold Pinter is famous for using the pause. The power of his drama exists in the subtext and undercurrents that occur in the silences. An audience cannot laugh unless the comedian gives them time to laugh by pausing. The 'rests' in music convey as much as the notes themselves.

If you want to be a powerful and compelling communicator, you have to pause.

Fears about pausing

A common worry about pausing is the fear of getting interrupted. I am often asked by clients in the training room, 'Surely, if I pause in a meeting, someone else will just leap in and hijack my point?' I'm afraid the answer to this is YES, they will – IF your energy is too low. If the energy is low, then listeners will feel bored, get frustrated and stop listening, and then of course they will want to interrupt.

But if your pause has dynamic energy beforehand and dynamic energy afterwards, then it is almost impossible to interrupt. The speaker stays in control of the room.

How do we stay in control during the pause?

The first way to do this is to use *connective words* – for example, 'so', 'now', 'then', 'however'. I like to think of these connective words as the verbal equivalent of a capital letter or an attention-grabbing headline at the start of a new thought or sentence.

The second way to do this is to use a vocal technique I call *up an octave*. Imagine you are playing the piano. At the end of a musical phrase, there is a rest. When the music recommences, it has gone up by an octave.

Likewise, when you start to talk again after a pause it is vital that you re-pitch your voice. Imagine that your voice is going up an octave. An octave is eight notes higher: that's a big jump. It feels unnatural and uncomfortable. But for the listener, it grabs and re-engages the attention: it's a big, bold capital letter at the beginning of a new thought. This starts to give your voice colour, music and variety. It's a piece of Mozart rather than a monotone. The patient is alive rather than flatlining.

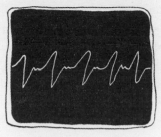
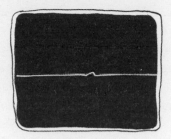

healthy and alive   close to death

This is what I mean:

'My team and I have a lot of experience in this area let me tell you about a similar client outsourcing project I led last year it was for a well-known telecoms company with offices in both Europe and the States and the chief operating officer was keen to make substantial savings in a very short space of time.'

There is no verbal punctuation here; rather, there are a number of different thoughts which have all run into one. No pause. For a listener, this is difficult to stay engaged with. *It's hard work. I won't listen.*

'My team and I have a lot of experience in this area. Let me tell you about a similar client outsourcing project I led last year. It was for a well-known telecoms company with offices in both Europe and the States. The chief operating officer was keen to make substantial savings in a very short space of time.'

This is slightly better. At least the four thoughts have been broken up into four sentences. There is the start of some structure and clarity for the listener. But not enough. *Still no pause or connectives. As a listener, there's a strong chance I'm zoning out.*

'**MY** team and I have a *huge* amount of experience in this area. *(pause)* **SO**, (pause) let me tell you about a similar client outsourcing project I led last year. (pause) *It* was for a *large* telecoms company with offices in both *Europe* and the *States. (pause)* **NOW** (pause) the *Chief Operating Officer* was keen to make substantial savings in a *very* short space of time.'

This is much better. There are five substantial pauses. There are two connectives. There is some emphasis on key words. The words in bold represent the voice being re-pitched up an octave. Result – there is music and variety in the voice. *It's interesting. I can't help but listen.*

So, for me, the ingredients of dynamic energy and pause working together are a potent and intoxicating combination.

Imagine a skiing beginner being given some basic equipment – some skis and poles – and then being told to take the chairlift to the summit of the mountain, dismount at the top of a red run, point their skis downhill and go.

Oh dear. That's scary. It won't be fun. It might even be ugly. There's going to be an accident. They might even end up being taken down on the blood wagon. It would be a crazy course of action. We would never attempt to ski without some basic lessons and technique.

Why, then, do so many of us attempt to communicate and speak in public without some basic lessons and techniques? OK, we're not going to end up in hospital if we do a bad presentation or experience a poor meeting; but it can be a miserable, confidence-bashing experience. Assumptions and judgements are made about us constantly. These assumptions and judgements are based on the verbal and visual cues we give, and on our communication style. *This team haven't got what it takes, this man is dull, this woman isn't ready for a* promotion, *this senior manager is dry, this partner is nervous*. These judgements are career-limiting.

And sometimes, the judgements can land you in court.

I'll never forget being told by my mum, 'Don't use that tone of voice with me,' when I was being particularly snarky as a teenager. We know how it feels to be condescended to, or spoken to in a dismissive or hostile manner.

There's a fascinating study by Nalini Ambadi, who looked at the conversations recorded between surgeons and patients.[*] The conversations had been pre-filtered into two groups – a group of surgeons who had been sued at least twice, and a group who had never been sued. Ambadi chose clips from the beginnings and the ends of conversations between both parties. (These are important because – like any form of communication – they set the tone of the conversation and leave lasting impressions on the patients.)

Ambadi removed the 'high-frequency sounds from speech that make words understandable'. All that was left was a form of noise that sounded like you were listening underwater – no words were audible. Only the intonation, speed, pitch and rhythm were left. She analysed the clips for qualities such as warmth, hostility, dominance and anxiety. She found that by using just those voice tones, she could predict which surgeons had been sued for malpractice and which had not. The doctors who had been sued sounded dominant, hostile and less empathetic – i.e., lower concern or anxiety in their voice. Those who had a warmer-toned conversational style had not been sued, *regardless of what*

---

* Nalini Ambadi et al., 'Surgeons' tone of voice: A clue to malpractice history', *Surgery*, Volume 132, Issue 1: 5–9, 2002.

procedures they'd performed or whether they'd made a mistake.

This is extraordinary stuff. Forty seconds' worth of content-free audio is enough to predict whether a doctor has been sued for malpractice or not.

Sandy Pentland has looked at the 'tone of voice' people use when pitching business plans.* He performed an experiment with mid-career executives pitching real business plans for a business plan competition:

> *It turns out you can estimate their ratings of each other*
> *. . . just by listening to their tone of voice. You didn't have*
> *to know anything about the business plan; you didn't*
> *have to know anything about the executives. It was*
> *how they delivered the plan that determined how it was*
> *rated. That's pretty amazing. Because these were not*
> *fools. These were executives in their mid-thirties – very*
> *successful. And yet they were listening to how excited the*
> *presenter was about the plan; they were not listening*
> *to the facts.*

What does all of this mean for us as speakers? Think about your objective in opening your mouth to speak. Are you trying to rile your audience? Do you want them to sue you? To commit bodily harm? Fire you? Not hire you? Never promote you?

Taking care over your verbal tone – using warmer, more vibrant tones rather than hostile, flat, monotone or dominant tones – will get your audience on your side.

---

* Alex ('Sandy') Pentland, 'Defend Your Research: We Can Measure the Power of Charisma', *Harvard Business Review*, January–February 2010.

So, just as a skiing beginner needs techniques to help him to ski safely down a mountain, we need techniques to help us communicate effectively – wherever we are, and whomever we are talking to. What matters is that we sell ourselves positively, and are in control of what others are thinking and feeling about us.

That's why the combination of dynamic energy and pausing is so potent. When these techniques are used properly, the audience doesn't see our nerves. They see confidence. Instead of someone looking wooden or awkward, they see someone looking relaxed and comfortable. They see someone who looks like they want to be there, a communicator who is enjoying themselves. Most importantly, our audience are listening to and enjoying every word we say.

Eye contact

Imagine being in a garden holding a hose. You're walking down a row of plants, spraying them, but none really gets a huge amount of water. Now imagine you have a watering can. You stop at each individual plant and give it your focus. That's the way to treat your audience. Move your gaze around so that each person in the room gets some direct attention.

Over the years I've had various push-backs to this advice: 'I don't want them to feel I'm staring them down.' 'What if they don't look back at me?' 'But I sometimes need to look away when I'm speaking to remember what to say.'

I'm not suggesting that you enter into a 'who blinks first dies' staring contest. And of course, when you need to think about your next point, *pause*, look away, and then come back to looking at a member of your audience. You'll be able to gauge if the audience is with you or if someone hasn't quite got your point. You'll build relationships.

Smiling

Remember Oullier's work on mirroring? If I smile at you, it's difficult not to smile back. It's easier to smile when you're speaking from personal experience. But that's for the next chapter.

Summary

Approximately 90 per cent of our verbal impact comes from what the audience see and hear, rather than what we say. This 90 per cent dictates how we feel about someone. Do we trust them? Do we have confidence in them? Can we connect with them?

To guarantee that the impact we have is the impact we want to have, we need:

Dynamic energy

Energy means projecting ourselves. We have to perform. It means we come across with conviction. It makes us look and sound like we want to be there.

We need to be 'in the zone'. It's hard work. Without energy, the audience has to work too hard and may switch off.

How to channel our energy

- direct eye contact
- bigger vocal volume
- throwing your voice up an octave

- using both hands to illustrate what we say – it helps us to look natural and confident
- pausing
- emphasis
- smiling.

How vocal energy helps

Use the range of your voice. The average person has three octaves in their voice. We use a tiny percentage of that when we're feeling nervous or under pressure. It's so much easier to stay listening to someone who uses the full register of her voice. Doctors who use positive, warm tones when they speak to patients don't get sued. The ones who use corrosive or harsh tones do. People who speak on one note are really hard to listen to. Watch out for ending your sentences on a higher note, though – making statements sound like questions is dangerous. It can undermine your authority.

How body language helps

By opening up, you not only project the impression of feeling comfortable and in control, but you also change the hormones your body releases. Your brain sends less cortisol (stress hormone) and more testosterone through your body. You look and sound confident, enthusiastic, captivating, comfortable, authentic and passionate. You also start to feel that way.

How pausing helps

Pausing gives you time to think. It makes you look and sound relaxed and comfortable. It gives the listener time to digest and absorb your messages and it turns a 'monologue' into what feels like a 'conversation'. As a rough rule, pause for three times longer and three times more often than feels comfortable. What feels like an eternity in your mind is usually less than a millisecond.

3:

TELLING THE STORY

This chapter shows you how to create compelling content that hooks your audience and keeps them with you.

Let's say I were to tell you about my last holiday.

If I started off saying, 'I'd like to tell you about three key aspects of my last holiday. The first is the travel and the transportation to the Bay Area region of California. The second is the spiciness of the Mexican food that one can imbibe while in those environs. The third is the heat one feels in California during a drought,' you'd be right for thinking, 'Who is this woman? Who speaks like that? Clearly she has no friends to visit or frankly anyone to go on holiday with. She is so boring!'

If I were really telling you about my holiday, it would be something along the following lines. 'It was fantastic. My friend Seth got married. There I was by the Golden Gate Bridge – in October – in a sundress and sunglasses. It was hot! My eyebrows were sweating from eating the spiciest Mexican food known to mankind. I was with all of my friends from high school. I loved it.'

I would tell you a story about a particular aspect of the holiday which would fit the message ('great holiday!').

But when we're in work mode it feels like we need the first version. This has structure. There are three key messages. The formal language comes flooding back.

I would never tell you that you shouldn't have three messages, or a structure to your speech. Of course you should. But I will tell you that you don't need to bang people over the head with it – and that there's a more interesting and memorable way to get your points across.

I'll never forget hearing about the start of the Arab Spring – when Tunisian street vendor Mohamed Bouazizi set himself on fire after being humiliated by a municipal officer. His weighing scales were confiscated and his wheelbarrow was turned over because he didn't have a vendor's permit or the money to bribe the police. This wasn't the first time – at age twenty-six he'd worked since he was ten and had, his friends and family say, been regularly harassed by police attempting to extort money. This time, he'd had enough. Perhaps it was the fact that the person who took his scales was a woman. He ran to the governor's office to demand justice. After the governor refused to see him – even though he threatened to set himself on fire – he bought a can of gasoline, stood in the middle of traffic in front of the governor's office, and set himself on fire. His action became the catalyst for protests and strikes across Tunisia and other parts of the Middle East.

Whenever you read about the Arab Spring you come across phrases like 'dissatisfaction with the rule of local government', 'economic decline', 'corruption', 'youth unemployment', 'extreme poverty', 'dissatisfied youth' and 'human rights violations'. The point of Mohamed's story is that it illustrates these phrases. It brings them to life. I can see the overturned wheelbarrow and weighing scales in my head. I can't, however, see 'corruption' or 'human rights violations' or 'dissatisfaction with the rule of local government'. There is nothing wrong with the words, but it is hard to think about 'dissatisfaction with the rule of local government' in a concrete way. Mohamed's brutal treatment by the regime and his subsequent self-immolation tell the story of part of the Arab Spring both brutally and memorably.

Mohamed's story paints a picture in your head. There are real people, real characters, real descriptions to latch on to.

We are addicted to stories. It is as though we have a story gene. A newspaper editor doesn't say to a journalist, 'Go and get me the facts and figures,' but instead, 'Go and get me the story.' It's why we love going to the theatre, or the cinema, or the opera. It's why we have piles of books next to our beds. It's why we take our e-readers on holiday.

Yet somehow, these stories get left behind when we go into presentation or speech mode. It's back to 'three key messages, two points I'd like to get across'.

The problem with 'three key messages' is that they are boring and predictable. Listeners turn off.

Stories, on the other hand, are compelling. They're memorable. And for the speaker, they're much easier to remember. Here's how to tell them.

Use 'I', not 'we'

I'm not saying that in every speech or presentation you give, you should take credit when others have done work. But while it may be clear in your head who you are talking about when you use 'we', it's unlikely that everyone else in the room knows who you mean. If you use 'we', you must define it.

The brilliant language commentator Ben Zimmer once

wrote a column about 'we' for the *New York Times* in which he lists some wonderful retorts to its usage:*

Rockwell Conkling, a New York senator after the US Civil War, took offence to President Rutherford B. Hayes' overuse of the word 'we'. The *St Louis Globe-Democrat* reported Conkling as saying, 'Yes, I have noticed there are three classes of people who always say "we" instead of "I". They are emperors, editors and men with a tapeworm.'

The Lone Ranger is famous for desperately asking his sidekick Tonto when surrounded by 'wild, screaming Indians', 'What will we do?' Tonto's reply: 'What do you mean, "we", Paleface?'

Or there is Curt Johnson, publisher of the magazine *December*, who wrote in 1966 of overhearing a student talk back to a college instructor: '"We"? You got a mouse in your pocket?'

---

* Ben Zimmer, 'We', *New York Times*, 1 October 2010.

While this use of 'we' is sometimes referred to as 'editorial', even editors come under fire for using the term. The prominent reformist preacher Thomas De Witt Talmage castigated them openly in 1875:

> *No honest man will ever write a thing for a newspaper in editorial or any other column that he would be ashamed to sign with the Christian name that his mother had him baptised with. They who go skulking about under the editorial 'we', unwilling to acknowledge their identity, are more fit for Delaware whipping posts than the position of public educators.*
>
> *It is high time that such hounds were muzzled.*[*]

There's even a word for those incapable of muzzling their 'we' tendencies: nosism. It comes from the Latin *nos* (which means 'we'), and means the practice of using 'we' when in fact we mean 'I'.

Sometimes, of course, we have to use 'we'. Apart from those alone on desert islands, no one does everything entirely by themselves. But if you use 'we', I want you to define who you mean. Are you including the person you've been working with? Does 'we' refer to everyone in your company? Or everyone in your department? Are *you* even involved? Are you saying that a particular member of your team, or the client's team, had the idea or did the work? Are you including in 'we' your assistant, or your boss? If so, then give them credit and use their names. If you did it together, then say something like 'Betsy and I think . . .' The more specific you get, the more informed your audience is.

Clients occasionally quote the phrase, 'There's no "I" in

---

* Thomas De Witt Talmage, *Around the Tea-Table*, 1874.

"team".' This is true. But as Leon in the Budweiser commercial said, 'Yeah, there ain't no "we" either.' (However, if you look closely, there is a 'me' in team.)

I'm not asking you to take credit when you haven't done the work. I'm not asking you to brag about something you haven't done. But I am asking you to raise your head above the parapet and take ownership for work you *have* done. I am asking you to give credit to other people when they've done the work, or been the catalyst for an idea. I'm also asking you to take credit for your own opinions.

The more specific you get, the clearer your message will be.

Using an undefined 'we' is lazy. It defers responsibility. It's hard to buy into your message.

Of course, if you are purposefully trying to obfuscate, then by all means ignore the advice above. But how often do you really want to confuse your audience? Or purposefully leave them in the dark? Or have them stop listening?

What's in a story?

What do all stories have? A beginning, a middle and an end. A good story takes you on a journey. This is not new. Aristotle talked about stories in his *Poetics* (350 BCE), when he said 'A whole is what has a beginning and middle and end.'

If I want my kids to do something they aren't keen on doing, like go on a seven-mile hike on their birthday, I have to tell them a story, usually about the last time we went on an unforgivably long walk. There is a famous one in my house about 'the time we all went on a ten-mile hike in Canada'. The story involves avoiding grizzly bears; a snow-

beginning   middle   end

ball fight in the middle of August as we crossed a mountain pass; walking around a lake that was supposed to take ten minutes and took three hours; getting lost in a swamp; sitting down for a break of trail mix and being swarmed by mosquitoes (again, and again and again); and one child refusing to pee on a tree by holding his bladder for so long that he nearly exploded at the site of the toilet at the end of the hike. It has a good narrative, with various details that can be expanded and compressed depending on time and my willingness to entertain.

It is extraordinary how long the kids can be distracted by the story of this hike. My husband has a similar technique – he likes to recount the plots of the scariest films he knows (think *Blair Witch Project*) as we walk through the failing light in forests. I am not so keen on this version of the technique as I hate scary movies, but it works for him. And they follow him like the Pied Piper, without a single word of complaint.

Mini-stories and anecdotes

For each of your messages, what anecdote can you tell? What mini-story illustrates the point you're making?

In the walking story I tell my kids, I'm making the point that while long walks can be difficult and, well, long, they sometimes are so crazy that they make a good story. One of my life tenets is that if you can get a good story out of a painful experience, it was worth it. My kids aren't really going to appreciate that sage piece of wisdom on its own. But wrapped up in the detail of the grizzly bear and the ever-present mosquito, they will grudgingly agree.

There's a great example of the use of a mini-story by a client who was giving a speech at an international law firm. Part of the speech involved making the point that there are long hours and weekends that get sacrificed, but since he found the work and the clients fascinating, it was worth it.

Said straight up, this point was going to sound pretty mundane. In one ear, out the other. He was going to look like every other lawyer forced to give up their lives for the office. So we landed on a story.

Jian had recently been asked to act as the tax lawyer on the case for a $700 million sale of a cyber security business. The deadline was so tight that it required the CEOs, private equity partners and Jian to hammer out the deal on a Saturday. This happened to be Jian's birthday. He hadn't mentioned this fact to anyone. He is a humble man who doesn't love the spotlight. However, he did tell the weekend security guard who showed Jian to the boardroom that he'd just turned forty-five. The security guard opened the door to the boardroom and announced to the assembled CEOs and partners: 'You're making this guy work on his birthday!'

Jian describes the moment of shocked silence with some hilarity as he then wished for the floor to miraculously open up and swallow him. 'And then it got even worse,' he says, 'as they all burst into singing "Happy Birthday". I've never been so embarrassed. I wanted to be there, it was such an exciting deal and I was properly interested in seeing it through.'

Anecdotes are ways to let little parts of our personality seep through. They prove a point in a way that only you can tell it, because it happened to you.

Analogies, similes and metaphors

Sometimes there isn't a mini-story that illustrates your point. Or the detail is dry and rather technical. That's where analogies, similes and metaphors are so brilliant.

Analogies compare one thing to another, to explain or clarify. They refer to something familiar or readily under-stood in order to illustrate and explain something more complex.

I love this example on Quora by Laura Copeland, of how science teachers might use analogies to help explain cell theory.[*]

> *Cells are tiny factories whose job is to take raw materials and produce a useable product (protein). The factory has the necessary plans or code (DNA) for its products. It also has an assembly line (the endoplasmic reticulum), a warehouse for storing the product (the Golgi apparatus) and a main office (the nucleus) that's walled off from the rest of the factory (with a nuclear membrane).*

A metaphor is a word or phrase that suggests that one thing is similar to another. They're a little fuzzier than analogies.

Here's Copeland's description of metaphors:

> *English teachers, on the other hand, are more likely to use **metaphor** to talk about cells. Unlike their colleagues in the science department, they aren't tasked with explaining a complicated process, so they're free to wax poetic about cells without having to make perfect logical sense:*

> * *Cancer cells are those which have **forgotten** how to die (from the prelude to a Harold Pinter poem 2002).*
> * *He donated sperm, and now his cells are **running around** in the wild.*
> * *I'm a **mosaic of cells** from my ancestors.*

A simile is a phrase that uses the words *like* or *as* to describe someone or something by comparing it with someone or something else that is similar.

---

[*] Laura Copeland, https://www.quora.com/Whats-the-difference-between-analogy-metaphor-and-simile.

Similes also work wonders for getting across technical detail.

Writer Marcus Geduld described the solar system with these similes on Quora:[*]

- *Planets orbited the sun like children dancing around a Maypole.*
- *The planets spun in their orbits, like ice-skaters circling a rink.*

Here's a few of these verbal pictures that I've come across that I like:

You're a kite dancing in a hurricane, Mr Bond. *Spectre*

I loved you head over handles, like my first bicycle accident – before the mouthful of gravel and blood, I swore we were flying. Sierra DeMulder

Boy, I got vision, and the rest of the world wears bifocals. Butch Cassidy

The life of man is like the swift flight of a single sparrow through the banqueting hall where you are sitting at dinner on a winter's day with your captains and counsellors. The Venerable Bede

Organizing my friends is like teaching cats to type. Richard Harris

The road of life is paved with flat squirrels who couldn't make a decision.

---

* Marcus Geduld, https://www.quora.com/What-is-a-good-metaphor-for-The-sun-in-which-planets-orbit-around.

Finding the perfect analogy is like balancing a muffin on a pencil. Joe Randazzo (@Randazzoj)

Cooler than the other side of the pillow.

All hat and no cattle. Texas saying

Procrastination is like a fine wine. It gets better with time.

Sometimes you have to feel the rain down the back of your neck. Getting uncomfortable makes you realize what you need to change. Swiss Grenadier

When I first started working at Bloomberg Television, it was like going over a waterfall in a barrel. I was pretty terrified, and had no idea if I'd survive my first day on air. A colleague once described his first month working at Microsoft as 'drinking from the firehose'. These analogies paint a clear picture of what you're talking about.

Characters

Most stories are about people. Your business is full of people. So, who are the people in your story? You are the narrator and the protagonist. But who are the other characters? Who are the goodies, the baddies, the heroes, the villains? What are their names? What job do they do? What's an interesting detail you could tell me about them? In my walk story, there are heroes (kids) and villains (bears, mosquitoes, me as the walk enforcer). In Jian's story the characters are the CEOs and partners and the porter. The villain in that story is time, which is against them all.

This allows you to get further away from 'we'. It shows your personal connections, your network. It shows how you manage a team.

What we tend to do is to talk about 'the client' or 'the organization' or 'the partners' or 'the team'. But this is bland and conceptual. Talking about the real characters and people brings you and your message to life. Which of these descriptions is more interesting?

'We built a trusted relationship with the client and sold a project worth £300,000.'

Or:

'Andrew, the COO, was a challenging character and notorious for his dislike and distrust of consultants. But I knew how important it was for me to build a strong relationship with him. It wasn't easy, and it didn't happen overnight, but over time he began to trust me. I discovered he was a wine buff and a keen hockey player. It was a good moment when he called me one weekend to discuss a problem with an IT implementation that was troubling him. A few days later he asked me to give him a proposal for a piece of work worth £300,000. That was three months ago. Andrew has just asked me to extend that piece of work and I'm now bringing in Ahmed and Emma to join Mila and Graham, doubling my team from two to four. I am really proud that because of the relationship I have built with Andrew, the project has doubled in size, scope and length.'

The colour and detail of the second example is much more engaging. It also contains more positive messages. This is vital for pitches, job interviews and promotions. This is when you show the level you're playing at. 'Last week when I had coffee with Duro Taben, the COO at Turnip Media, he told me that the strategy I'd delivered for him on expanding his work in Latin America was better than what he expected from a firm twice our size.'

Descriptions

Here's a little exercise. Close your eyes and think about one of your grandparents. Most of us, when we do this, see a picture. Charlotte's is of Granny McDougall, sitting in a

faded floral chair, smoking a cigarette in a draughty Norfolk kitchen. Granny McDougall died in 1977. This picture is nearly forty years old. But it is seared into her memory. We think in pictures. Think of Dickens' descriptions of Victorian London or Emily Brontë's descriptions of Heathcliff on the moor. Think *Alice in Wonderland*. Children's books are full of pictures and illustration.

The more visual you make your content, the more memorable you and your message become. But you only need a few key words to place those pictures in your audience's brain. 'We got lost by a lake with trees just taller than we could see over.' 'There was snow in August at the peak of the mountain pass – suddenly we all had to pull out our fleeces to put over our T-shirts!' In Jian's story, he says, 'I can still hear the scrape of four boardroom chairs against the floor and pens dropping on the table as these very senior colleagues wearing khakis and collared long-sleeve shirts leapt up and started singing to me.'

Using characters and descriptions allows you to personalize your content. It helps you to present yourself in three dimensions. The audience starts to understand why it's important for you to open your mouth in the first place.

Facts and emotions

Every story has facts. You might have numbers, profits or other metrics to report. This is all fine. What makes your speech stand out is when you attach an emotion to the fact. 'I'm really proud that Sara brought in three new clients this quarter. It shows how my team is getting behind the growth strategy. I'm delighted that . . . I'm worried that . . . I'm pleased that . . .'

Emotion allows us to see your personal opinion. As you move forward in your career, it's your opinion that matters.

Jian was horrified that there was so much attention on him. 'I was mortified. I hate being the centre of attention. I literally wanted the floor to open up beneath me and suck me inside, like Dory and Marlin getting eaten by the whale in *Finding Nemo*.' It makes the story much more touching to reveal his human side. Others would have reacted differently, and this shows his personality.

Emotion as a hook

Attach one emotion to each of your points. It's a great way to grab the audience.

It's also an easy way to start your speech, meeting or phone conversation. 'I'm so pleased you could join me.' 'I'm looking forward to telling you about . . .'

Message

What is your message? This sounds obvious, but why are you opening your mouth to speak? If there isn't a point you need to make, then stay silent. Sometimes, when time is short, you just need to get it out there.

We hear the spoken word only once, so keeping the message as simple as possible helps to make it memorable. And, of course, less is more.

The eminently quotable Mark Twain once said, 'I didn't have time to write a short letter, so I wrote a long one instead.' Spoken words can feel the same. If it is all feeling a little long, then just get to the point.

I once heard an economist speak about the financial future, and midway through her speech she realized that she had been allowed less time than she thought in which to make her points. 'Well,' she said, 'as my mom tells me, I'm just going to have to cut it and shut it.' She left the audience wanting more.

Matthew Barzun, US Ambassador to the UK, sometimes quotes a Kentucky politician (in turn quoting his Baptist preacher) when he says to remember 'the 5 Bs – "Be Brief, Brother. Be Brief."'

All of this means that you are not hiding behind a mask, but allowing your personality to emerge. We meet YOU. As a result, your authority, impact and profile go shooting up. By allowing us to build a relationship with you, we engage with and remember your message. This has a huge impact on your visibility and profile.

Jargon

Every professional tribe has its own language: management consultants, doctors, architects, lawyers, teachers, scientists, headhunters, film producers, firefighters. They all use words which have meaning only to those within the clique.

There are many problems with these linguistic subsets.

Other people don't speak the language. One very cold February morning in my gutted house, huddled with my builder and architect over cups of lukewarm instant coffee, I found myself, not for the first time, drifting off as they discussed

the date for 'installation of the moving elements'. Moving elements? Perhaps, I assumed, it was another joint project they were working on. No! They were agreeing the date for putting in the sliding glass and folding wooden doors in my own house. Turns out the date was rather sooner than I had expected, and I was supposed to be providing the aforementioned door products imminently.

Sometimes they may literally not speak your language. One client told me about a pitch they'd recently won. Let's call the pitched company the Bank of Bishkek. At the actual pitch there was a forty-five-minute discussion about the meaning of 'support'. Does it mean people? Time? How much of both? Likewise, 'resource'. Does 'resource' mean money or people, the Bank of Bishkek wanted to know? Or something else entirely?

You offend people. The *Financial Times*'s Lucy Kellaway gives her 'Golden Flannel' prize every January for exceptional use of 'corporate guff'. One award she gives is for the best euphemisms for being fired – Nokia 'managed for value', HSBC 'demised' its managers, Reuters staff were 'transitioned out of the company'. ABN Amro fired 1,000 people to 'further enhance the customer experience' and EY 'looked forward to strengthening our alumni network'. Imagine how you'd feel as a demised, transitioned, new alumnus.

No one knows what the words mean any more. Lucy Kellaway's 'Chief Obfuscation Champion' is given to the 'CEO who never opens his or her mouth without a blue streak of guff pouring out'. In 2014, Rob Stone, CEO of Cornerstone, received the award for writing, 'As brands build out a world footprint, they look for the no-holds-barred global POV that's always been part of our wheelhouse.'[*]

In 2015, when Apple CEO Tim Cook apologized for the privacy of celebrities being breached on iCloud, he said: 'When I step back from this terrible scenario . . . I think about the awareness piece. I think we have a responsibility to ratchet that up. That's not really an engineering thing.'[†] What is an awareness piece? How would one ratchet it? What on earth is he talking about?

Something unpleasant happens to your face. It's very difficult to buy into jargon. Quite often, the more difficult management words take longer to come out of your mouth. Your face also turns into a rather motionless, emotionless wall. It's very difficult to smile and connect with someone when discussing 'the tools in your wheelhouse' or 'leveraging opportunities and synergies'.

Jargon	Replace with
leverage	use
going forward	in the future
bandwidth	ability/time
the 'insert word' piece	the 'insert word'
resource	people or money
competencies	abilities
geographies	countries
processes	Be specific! What processes?

---

* Lucy Kellaway, 'Gongs for guff that reach new levels of flannel', *Financial Times*, 5 January 2014.
† Lucy Kellaway, 'And the Golden Flannel of the year award goes to . . .', *Financial Times*, 4 January 2015.

Julia Streets, CEO of Streets Consulting, a financial communications firm, has written a brilliant book called *The Lingua Franca of the Corporate Banker* in which she describes her journey to collect the most offensive jargon known to management mankind. Her glossary lists five hundred items. She's placed the worst offenders on a 'Lingua Franca Podium of Irritation.'*

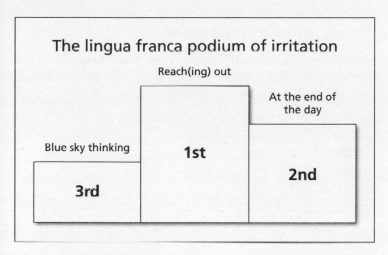

I recently conducted a highly unscientific survey of my Facebook friends' most hated business jargon. I was astonished by the response – from the worlds of politics and culture to business and sport, jargon gets people really, really cross. I've added to those my contacts hated a few more examples of overused buzzwords highlighted by Houston PR's Hamish Thompson in his 'Buzzsaw'†. I've taken the liberty of creating a word cloud with them.

---

* Julia Streets, *The Lingua Franca of the Corporate Banker*, 2012.
† http://www.prbuzzsaw.com.

cascade

methodology   forward planning

action   it's got legs   reach out

task   blue sky thinking

going forward   paradigm shift

                                        Key Performance Indicators

reinvent the wheel   overarching   transition

de-layer   reconnect   incentivize   call to action
          ecosystem   manage expectations

bandwidth   evangelist   strategize   out of pocket

robust   engagement double-click on that   deep dive

empower   value proposition   align goals

market-leading   big data   synergies   wheelhouse

global provider   impactful

work around   robust procedures   leverage

bottom up   consultation   touch base

bandwidth   pick your brain   top down
          touch base   lean in
stewardship   seek consensus   secret sauce

take offline   update   granularity

park this issue   learnings   net net   flag up   pivot

fulfilment issues   step back   dominate

demising core competency   politically correct

next-generation   visioning

pilot   edgy   interface   double click on that

          getting buy in   I hear you

let's unpack that   curate   low hanging fruit

circle back   onboarding

I believe that, in business, the spoken and written word can get confused and we can end up sounding overly formal and wordy. The spoken word is not good for transmitting vast amounts of information. But it is good for connecting with people and building an argument. Telling the story takes the audience on a journey, bringing to life even the most technical content.

Telling stories is part of human existence. Why make it difficult, both for you and your audience, by reverting to 'three key points I'd like to make'?

Summary

Beginning, middle and end – think of these instead of your points 1, 2 and 3. Take the listener on a journey through your thoughts.

Using 'I'

We want to hear *your* beliefs and opinions, not 'we believe' or 'our opinion is'. The ability to stick your head above the parapet and take ownership for your beliefs gives you authority and confidence. When you tell the audience about your personal experience, it means that they buy into your personal knowledge and expertise. Your status goes shooting up. If you use 'we' without being either the Queen or infested with tapeworm, you have to define who 'we' is.

Pictures/images/people

When we're with our friends, we relish telling stories and anecdotes. We paint pictures with words and enjoy the little details. When we talk about business, we often forget to do this. However, the way our memory works is that we remember things visually. So an image or a vivid description helps others to remember our message. Tell me who the characters are and take a moment to describe them, or the scene you found yourself in.

Facts and emotions

Not only do I want to hear the facts, but the emotion behind the facts. What excites you, what worries you? What are you thrilled about? What are you proud of? This lets us in. We can begin to build a relationship with you. You become real and are emotionally connected rather than just a talking head.

Language

Use plain language. What words would you use with an intelligent teenager? Quite often the audience doesn't always get the jargon, even if they pretend they do. Even if everyone in the room speaks business/medical/HR/legalese, remember that the best speakers don't use it. Ever. Even if they can.

Analogies and examples

We use these all the time in our non-working lives. An analogy is a brilliant way of adding colour and making the complex seem simple, especially for drier or more technical details. Using real-life examples helps to keep things concrete rather than general or conceptual. It is much more difficult for us to connect with concepts and facts.

Message

What is your message? This sounds obvious, but why are you speaking at all? Keeping the message as simple as possible ensures clarity. And – of course – less is more.

4:

THE SCIENCE BEHIND THIS STUFF

Stories can literally put us on the same wavelength

Ever felt that you 'are on the same wavelength' as someone else? Uri Hasson and Greg Stephens have measured this phenomenon, which is known as 'neural coupling'. Lauren Silbert, one of the graduate students in their lab at Princeton, recorded an unrehearsed story about a disastrous high school prom involving two suitors, a fistfight, and a car accident. A group of twelve people listened to her recording while lying in a brain-scanning machine undergoing fMRI (a brain scan that examines where blood is flowing to detect areas of activity).

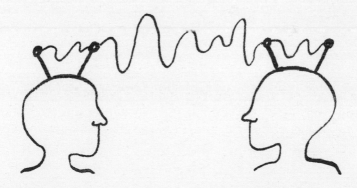

The results showed that the more the listeners understood the story, the more closely their brain responses matched up with those of the person telling the story. Dr Hasson told me in email correspondence about the experiment: 'While in many brain areas the responses in the listener's brain lagged after the responses in the speaker's brain, in some areas the listener's brain responses anticipated the responses in the speaker's brain, as if the listener were able to predict and anticipate the speaker's next utterances. The stronger the similarity between the speaker's brain responses and the listener's brain responses, in particular in these anticipatory brain areas, the better the communication.'

Hasson described the mind-meld phenomenon as: 'two tightly coupled brains communicating well. It's that feeling you get that you just click with someone. It's almost visceral. You can finish their sentences. You just know you're on the same wave. By the way you can get similarly strong feelings when you're not in sync with someone. Sometimes you can just feel it when someone's talking and you're not getting it. Your brains aren't coupling.'*

What a great thought it is that, while you are speaking, the audience's brain pattern will begin to reflect yours as people get swept up in your story.

---

* Uri Hasson, 'Defend Your Research: I Can Make Your Brain Look Like Mine', *Harvard Business Review*, December 2010.

Stories can cause the audience to take action

Paul J. Zak has done research on the neurobiology of storytelling. He's shown that character-driven stories with emotional content and narrative tension result in better understanding and better recall. They can also result in the audience taking positive action.

Zak shows a video of a true story about a two-year-old boy called Ben. Ben is dying of brain cancer. We are told this by Ben's father, as we watch Ben happily playing in the background. Ben's father says it's difficult to be happy around Ben because he knows he's only got two months left to live. In the end Ben's father resolves to find the strength, for the sake of his son, to be genuinely joyful until the moment when Ben takes his last breath. In Hollywood this would be known as the 'hero's journey'. The story has a classic narrative arc. It starts with something new and surprising, tension increases, there is soul-searching to overcome the crisis, and a resolution at the end.

Zak found that the two emotions felt by those watching the video were distress and empathy. He also measured the physical manifestations of these emotions through the audience's heart rates, skin temperature and respiration. He took blood samples of the amount of cortisol and oxytocin released by the brain into the bloodstream. (The more distressed you are, the more cortisol you release, and the more care, connection and empathy you feel, the more oxytocin you release.) After watching the video the audience were given the opportunity to donate money to a stranger they couldn't see and to a charity associated with child illness. Those in a heightened emotional state gave money. They were being paid $20 to participate in the study, and the most affected of them were giving half of it away. **Zak's lab had 'hacked' their brains with stories to motivate them to be more cooperative.**

Zak says: 'We discovered that, in order to motivate a desire to help others, a story must first sustain attention – a scarce resource in the brain – by developing tension during the narrative. If the story is able to create that tension then it is likely that attentive viewers/listeners will come to share the emotions of the characters in it, and after it ends, likely to continue mimicking the feelings and behaviors of those characters.'[*]

---

[*]   See http://greatergood.berkeley.edu/article/item/how_stories_change_brain and
https://hbr.org/2014/10/why-your-brain-loves-good-storytelling/.

There are parts of the audience's brain you need to light up

Roy H. Williams is a marketing guru and the founder of the Wizard Academy Institute outside Austin, Texas. He isn't a neuroscientist but he's written a great deal about the brain and effective communication. Not far from him in Austin is Brian Massey, the 'Conversion Scientist', who has used Williams's teaching about the brain in his work on driving website traffic and helping companies increase their sales.

Both of them point out two important areas of the brain. Broca's area – just in front of your left ear – is what Williams calls the 'theatre critic of the imagination, the part of the human mind that anticipates and ignores the predictable'.[*] As Massey told me in 2016, 'it's the part of the brain that is responsible for taking words and translating them into

---

* Roy H. Williams, *Secret Formulas of the Wizard of Ads*, 1999, p. 50.

the meaning they have and casting them onto the visual spatial sketchpad in our brain. If you are listening to a speech, this sketchpad is where you can imagine doing something that the speaker is saying.'

Just behind the left ear is Wernicke's area. Its primary job is to take nouns and attach them to the memories of what the noun means. If I say 'broccoli', it is Wernicke's area that brings the images and experiences that you have of broccoli to mind so that you know what 'broccoli' means. These areas work together via a high-speed network of nerves (called the arcuate fasciculus) to decode words and apply meaning.

Massey says that if we were monitoring the audience's brains, we'd like to see Broca's and Wernicke's areas light up during a speech so that we knew the audience was thinking about our messages and taking action. Broca's area is the part that tells you the difference between grass blowing in the wind and grass being stomped on by a tiger. It filters out the predictable and highlights the strange or unexpected. Massey calls it the 'bouncer' that stops action being taken by the motor association cortex, which sits behind your fore-head. If Massey said 'Pick your nose in this lecture', Broca's area would light up because this is unexpected. It would ask Wernicke if this is a good idea. Wernicke would recall that picking your nose is socially embarrassing, this memory is displayed on the sketchpad, and most people would not do it. If he said 'Raise your hand if you have questions', this would likely be rejected by Broca as expected. Wernicke might not be disturbed. No image would appear in the motor cortex. Most people don't raise their hands in a presentation, even if they have questions.

Broca's area also does something more insidious when it

filters out the predictable. If your brain has heard a phrase or piece of jargon too many times, Broca's area discounts it. It tunes out. Yet another reason to steer away from jargon!

How do we, as speakers, sneak past Broca's area?

Think 'idea porn' (a term I once heard Mark Borkowski use when he discussed what triggers you need to get people to pay attention and make a decision).* In short, he says: make it funny, sexy, cute, shocking, illuminating, spectacular, controversial, topical and with a touch of *schadenfreude* (the pleasure we sometimes derive from another person's misfortune).

Relevant and emotional words are in Wernicke's area, says Massey. To get past Broca's area, use unexpected words that are inconsistent with what the audience is expecting.

* Edie Lush, '40 per cent of online advertising misses the target: here's why', The Week.co.uk, 19 May 2014, http://www.theweek.co.uk/technology/58578/40-of-online-advertising-misses-the-target-heres-why.

Summary

Stories can put you on the same wavelength as someone else. Literally. Telling stories makes you resonate with people's brains through a phenomenon called 'neural coupling'. Scientists have shown that when someone gets swept up in your story, their brain pattern starts to match yours. When you are really connecting with someone, their brain pattern can even predict yours. Being on the same wavelength is a real thing.

Character-driven stories with a narrative arc, starting with something new and surprising, containing tension and soul-searching, with resolution at the end keep the audience engaged and cause them to feel empathy with the speaker. Scientists have shown that it is possible to get audiences to take action when their emotional responses are heightened.

Our brains filter out the predictable. They highlight the strange and unexpected. This means that as speakers, we need to get past the 'bouncers' in the audience's brains. Use words that surprise the audience. Use emotion. Make it shocking or controversial. Ditch the jargon.

5:

PREPARING FOR AN INTERVIEW

This chapter will help you prepare for a job, project or university interview, as well as any meeting that <u>feels</u> like an interview.

When I was twenty-six I moved from Washington, D.C. to New York City. While looking for the job of my dreams, I temped as a PA in an insurance company. This was in the days before high-speed elevators. The elevator from the fiftieth floor to the ground floor took about two minutes.

Not long after starting, I found myself waiting next to a guy from the adjoining office, which was called Omega Advisors. We struck up a conversation and by the time we'd

got to the ground floor we'd discussed Oasis vs Pulp (it was the nineties, and my new acquaintance was Scottish), the West Village, where we both lived, what on earth Omega Advisors was (a hedge fund) and – as we neared Floor 3 – the fact that my dream was to become a political analyst. It turned out that Dr Hall – my elevator companion – needed someone to help him in his role as chief economist. Two days later I had an official interview with the rest of the team, and I started the job the following month.

What's the point of that real-life elevator pitch story?

A job interview starts well before you walk into the room.

From your initial point of contact – phone call or email – think about the impression you want to make, and what you want the listener to take from your words. My coaching colleague Hugo Simpson stresses that when writing any email, you should think: what action do I want the reader to take? What impression do I want to leave with them?

Physical preparation: some tips, dos and don'ts

Once you're at the interview:

Do: walk up a few flights of stairs to get energized and wake up your body.

If you are feeling nervous:

Do: some 'power poses' in the toilet cubicle before you get started. Head straight up. Imagine you are a puppet on a string. Shoulders back and down. Put your hands on your hips and keep your feet hip-width apart. You can do some mindful breathing while you stand like this for at least two minutes. Breathe in, and breathe out *one*, breath in, breathe out *two* . . . all the way up to ten. Repeat!

Don't: Sit, hunch your shoulders and read your phone – creating 'text neck'. If you sit while you're waiting, have shoulders back and down and your head straight up. You can still fiddle with your phone.

NO   YES

Do: be pleasant to everyone you meet in the building. You don't know who you are going to stand next to in the elevator. You don't know how friendly the receptionist is with the interviewer. When I had to interview the temporary replacements for my job in the insurance company before I left to work for Omega Advisors, I used my friend Tanisha, who ran the front desk, as my secret weapon. 'What were they like in the waiting room? Were they polite to you?' Basic emotional intelligence: it costs nothing to be nice.

Now that you are physically prepared, make sure you don't faff around when you get called in. If you have a coat, put it over your left arm, which will also be holding your handbag/briefcase. When you meet the interviewer you'll be ready to give them a firm, not bone-crushing, handshake with your right hand.

Verbal preparation

Despite the fact that you are not the one in charge of asking the questions, imagine that you are. A great way to start any interview is to put yourself in the frame of mind of the host. Imagine it's a dinner party and you're the one inviting everyone in. So, 'how will I make this person feel more comfortable around me?' The answer is to divulge something about yourself.

But what? Before I go into any pitch or meeting in which I'm asking somebody to do something for me (which in essence is an interview – are they going to give me the job?), I spend time thinking about the stories I'm going to bring into the room.

What did you do at the weekend? What film did you see that you really liked? What have you just read in the newspaper that surprised you? What work of art is hanging on the wall? Is there a TV showing the news in the waiting room? What story did you see? When asked 'How are you?', use this as an opportunity to bring out the story.

You can use nearly anything as a kicking-off point. The more comfortable you are once the job-related questions get going, the better off you'll be. The way to get comfortable is to get into safe territory – by telling a story about something that happened to you.

I've heard this called 'small talk' or 'breaking the ice'. I think that denigrates a technique that is actually the foundation of building a relationship: connecting with another real person about something tangible.

I've had clients say to me, 'But no one wants to know how you really are. It's just something you say.' Really? Then why not hire a robot instead? As the sports agent and writer Mark McCormack said, 'All things being equal, people will do business with a friend; all things being unequal, people will still do business with a friend.'* You probably aren't going to turn the interviewee into a friend in the course of an interview, but what you can do is start to create a more three-dimensional version of yourself than what exists on your CV. The more personal information you give up front, the more of a human being you become in the eyes of those interviewing you, and the more difficult you then are to ignore.

Steer clear of discussing the weather, unless you were pelted by hail the size of golf balls or had to walk through a snowstorm or ring of fire to get to the interview. The point of opening your mouth at this point is to allow the interviewer to get to know you. You're building a relationship with him or her. You want them to know that you're comfortable with people.

But of course you aren't in transmission mode. In your pauses (see Chapter 2), check in with the audience – in this instance, your interviewer. Are they nodding? Is there an opportunity to ask them a question back? Has she seen that film? What did he do at the weekend?

Sometimes people take a bit longer to warm up. In which case, keep at it. The longer you can keep the interview from

---

* I'm grateful to campaigns expert Michael Hayman for pointing out this quotation to me.

'officially starting', the better. Sometimes I tell my clients to see how long they can keep the interviewer standing up. Five minutes? Ten minutes?

Of course this isn't just useful for job interviews. One of my favourite examples of the success of this technique comes from a Swiss client. A former cycling champion, Markus was responsible for managing the CHF 20 million relationship for his company, a financial consulting group, with a global investment bank. Every few years the contract had to be renegotiated – not by the people who did the work, but by an operative within the accounts department. Markus told me he was still on a second-name basis with his colleague, Mr Frei. Markus is a warm, interesting, likeable character, but the experience of talking money with Mr Frei was so stressful that he found himself going into 'negotiation mode' with Mr Frei straight away. The relationship was deteriorating, and the Swiss bank wanted to cut the work Markus's company was doing for them. If Markus couldn't land the deal by the end of the week it was going to get kicked upstairs – the COO of Markus's company was going to have to get involved, which wasn't great for Markus. By all accounts, Mr Frei did not sound like a friendly character. He was 'trained in negotiation tactics', had a perfect poker face and had perfected the art of 'zero response' (he was good at pauses!).

Markus and I worked on the warm-up. Every time he went to the bank, Mr Frei met him at the front door and walked him through the bond and equities trading floors and up the stairs to the meeting room. We worked on the stories Markus would tell. We worked on questions Markus could ask Mr Frei, although Markus assured me that Mr Frei didn't have any life, wouldn't disclose anything and would just shut Markus down. I challenged Markus to find out two things about Mr Frei before they sat down to negotiate.

The email I got from Markus tells the entire story:

The client meeting with Mr Frei actually went well – I spent twenty-five minutes discussing personal things (He has a girlfriend, he started to bike last year, he bought a new bicycle this year, they go biking in western Switzerland – so actually I got more than two things!), and then we dove into [the] document I sent him. No agreement yet, but he accepted my initial position and isn't escalating it to our bosses. He did not fall off the chair or close me down. And he asked me to call him Roland.

If Markus can do it before negotiating a multimillion Swiss franc deal, then you can do it before your job interview.

Once you do sit down, you'll feel more relaxed, you'll have shown the interviewer a different side of yourself and you'll have made yourself memorable.

People form 60 to 80 per cent of their initial opinion about a new person in less than four minutes – so spend the first few minutes building a relationship with your interviewer. * Don't be afraid to keep the conversation going on non-work-related topics. You'll get down to the nitty-gritty soon enough.

---

* Ray Birdwhistell, *Kinesics and Context: Essays on Body Motion Communication*, 1970.

Here come the questions!

Listen to the questions. This sounds obvious, but a regular criticism of a non-successful candidate is that he or she 'didn't actually answer the question'. To give yourself more time to answer, repeat the question back. Literally, word for word. 'So, why do I want to work here?' This will show the interviewer that you heard them while also giving you time to think, and – if necessary – allowing you to clarify anything you are not sure about.

While there are millions of potential questions that can be asked, there are a few of the more general kind that often come up. Here's how to deal with them.

Basic opening questions

Tell me about yourself. Why do you want to work here? Where do you see yourself in ten years' time? What are you passionate about? Why do you want to be a digital over-lord / lawyer / oyster-floater / student in this university / mall Santa / doctor / shredded cheese authority / consultant / corporate magician?

These are great opening questions. They are the equivalent of receiving a serve on the tennis court. Here you go – over to you.

While they are composed of different words, they are basically the same question. They are asking you to tell a story.

The point of this story is to answer the question so that the interviewer thinks that everything you've done leading up to this moment makes you a terrific person for the job.

Example: I had a client who worked in child protection

services in Scotland. After a long stint in a government-funded organization, he decided he wanted to apply for a job in a national charity as director of children's services. We worked on his first answer – imagining the question as 'Why do you want this job?' – in the following way:

> *I'm passionate about protecting some of the most vulnerable people in society. I've spent nearly two decades working with children of separated or divorced parents who have been unable to see one of their parents. I've seen up close the damage that these kids endure after their parents end up in court fighting for the right to stop their partner from seeing their child. So, I've made it my life's ambition to help children like these. I've run centres where separated parents can visit with their children in safe environments. I've run an agency in Scotland responsible for working with the courts, mediation agencies and parents. I'm proud to have been part of a government-sanctioned team developing policies across the UK to ensure that the needs of the child were put first in court cases. I'm delighted that as a result of the policies this group created, fewer cases end up in court. Now I'd like to use my experience to help vulnerable children – from refugees to runaways – across the country.*

Behavioural questions

Behavioural questions are ones that start with 'Tell me about a time when . . .'

Tell me about a time when . . . you faced a big obstacle in your career? You had to get someone to do something they didn't want to do? You had to make a team pull together?

Jason Warner, a former recruiting executive at Google and Starbucks and the founder of RecruitingDash, a recruiting metrics software company, has a great formula for how to answer these.*

The acronym he uses is SARI (Situation, Action, Result, Interesting Feature). You can remember it by thinking: *if I don't remember this I'm going to be SARI.*

> **S**ituation: Describe the situation in a way that gives the listener some context. Be specific with the name of where this took place, and the issue that is at hand.
>
> **A**ction: What did you do? This is the moment to use 'I', not 'we'. If others helped you, it is fine to recognize their role – but this is really your moment. The audience is looking for specific behaviours here.
>
> **R**esult: What was the positive result? Give some numbers or business metrics here.
>
> **I**nteresting Feature: Something special or memorable about the story. Add in some emotion – why are you proud of this moment? Why are you telling me about it?

Say the question is: 'Tell me about a time you had to lead a team through a difficult moment.'

> **Situation:** I was recently in Peru leading a team producing a series of interviews with CEOs, artists and academics, to be shown on a corporate website requiring a very quick turnaround time. The interviews went really well, but due to the poor wifi

---

* http://blog.penelopetrunk.com/2007/03/13/google-guy-ace-the-behavioural-interview/

we fell behind schedule getting them uploaded. The client started sending frosty emails because he'd been promised twenty-five interviews and we had only delivered him ten. My team was demotivated, because they'd worked really hard to deliver quality content, and weren't pleased with the criticism.

Action: First of all I called the client and spoke to him on the phone. I find a little personal conversation goes a long way towards defusing hostility! I explained the situation and that we still had a couple of key interviews to record, after which we'd move to a different location where I'd already checked out the wifi speed. It wasn't as beautiful as the spot we were shooting in, but it would halve turnaround times for the interviews.

Result: The client was relieved I'd been so responsive, and didn't mind that the second shot was far less scenic. He was delighted with the extra five interviews we produced in the new location, and made a special effort to promote them in the company. A couple of the interviews went viral and got up to 90,000 views within a day.

Interesting Feature: My client still talks about the moment that I managed to save their coverage of a live event from failing, and recommended me to someone else in the company. I went on to produce similar events in Chile and Argentina.

Brainteasers

— How many pennies would it take to reach the top of the Empire State Building in New York?

- How many times heavier is a Blue Whale than an anchovy?
- Why is there fuzz on a tennis ball, but not on a squash ball?
- What's a good product for Visa to launch next?
- How do they make M&Ms?

Some people rejoice at a brainteaser. Others do not. There are books written on how to answer these questions. This is not one of those books. I include these questions because they have a very important communications angle. They are still part of a conversation.

Answering a brainteaser is the verbal equivalent of 'showing your work' in a maths test. These are designed to discover how you think. They're sometimes designed to figure out how you think when you don't know everything you need to know to reach the answer.

William Poundstone has written a book called *How Would You Move Mount Fuji?* and offers some sage advice.

They really expect you to walk them through your whole way of reasoning. And even if you end up not getting the right answer, they can be very impressed by some of the approaches you toss out there. In solving any real-world problem in business, you basically have to go through this process of brainstorming some ideas that aren't going to work out. So if you can show that you can do that – even with one of these [mind-bending] problems – that gives them a lot of useful information, even if you don't actually come up with the answer. [*]

* William Poundstone, *How Would You Move Mount Fuji?*, 2003.

Don't forget to ask some questions yourself

Do you mean the pennies stacked up on top of each other, in piles? Or laid out so you see the circles side by side? Peanut M&Ms, or plain?

Just like any other interview question, the more you can get a conversation going, the better off you are. These ones need to show how clever you are, so the questioning needs to stay on topic. Do some scribbling. Then talk your interviewer through your thought process.

Turn your CV into stories

There are thousands of potential interview questions. You can't prepare for all of them. But you can prepare for many of them.

Take your CV and look at what you've done. Each job should inspire a cluster of stories that you can tell for the behavioural and opening questions. Some stories will work for more than one question. This is fine.

Do you need to rehearse them? Yes, out loud. Use your phone to record your answers and watch them back. When I'm training clients who are going for job or promotion interviews, we have at least three sessions going through the questions. I've got the camera going a lot of the time.

But doesn't this end up sounding rehearsed? Think about the stories from your holidays, or your childhood. They are rehearsed in the sense that you know them, because you lived them, and you've told them several times in a way you know works for the listener. Your career stories are the same. If you tell them in the way you lived them, they will be an authentic reflection of aspects of your personality and job history.

When the singer Taylor Swift was asked in an interview with *GQ* if she was 'calculating' with her career, she responded, 'You can be accidentally successful for three or four years. Accidents happen. But careers take hard work.'*

With all questions, check in with your interviewer

If you are a bit unclear about what a question requires of you, ask for clarification.

Use eye contact. Ask some questions back: would the interviewer like to hear more? Is this what he or she was getting at with their question?

Summary

The interview starts well before you walk into the room. From your initial point of contact – whether by email or phone call – think about the impression you want to make and what you want the listener to take from your words.

How you say it

Come into the interview with positive energy. Think of a few interesting non-work/school related stories to bring into the room – what you did at the weekend, something you've read

---

* Chuck Klosterman, 'Taylor Swift on "Bad Blood," Kanye West, and How People Interpret Her Lyrics', 15 October 2015. I'm grateful to Penelope Trunk's blog for pointing this out to me. http://blog. penelopetrunk.com/2015/10/22/there-are-only-3-types-of-interview-questions-here-are-your-answers/

in the newspaper or a book you're reading. When you're asked 'How are you?', bring the story out.

Put yourself in the mind of the host of the meeting. You want the interviewer to feel comfortable around you. Try to stay standing, and talk to the interviewer for a few minutes. Speak personally. It'll help you relax a bit and show the interviewer that you're confident and multifaceted. Ask some questions of the interviewer. Show them your human side, the parts of you not reflected anywhere on your CV.

Once you do sit down, use the techniques from Chapter 2 to keep up the dynamic energy.

Listen to the questions. To give yourself more time to answer a question, repeat it back to the interviewer. This will also show the questioner you're hearing them. Keep direct eye contact with the interviewer. Look away when you're thinking – or pausing – but then come back to the eyes. Keep the volume up, and emphasize your words. Smile!

What you say

Start strong: 'I'm really delighted to be here.' Speak personally – using 'I', not 'we'.

'I'm fascinated by this question.' 'I'm really interested in this.' 'I'm proud of this achievement.' This lets the interviewer in and allows him or her to begin building a relationship with you.

Ask questions back to the interviewer. 'Am I making sense?' 'Do you want to hear any more about that?' 'Have I answered that question for you?'

Use examples to illustrate your points. Rather than saying, 'I'm good at taking the initiative,' give a real example of a time you took the initiative.

Have a list of questions you'd like to ask the interviewer. Do your homework, both on the company/institution and the interviewer. That's what the web is for!

Practise. Use your phone's video camera to rehearse your answers to questions, and watch them back to see if you made your point well.

6:

CASE STUDY: THE JOB INTERVIEW

Stephen was a director at one of the 'big four' professional services firms in London. He was a technology and IT specialist with over fifteen years' experience. During this time he had established a large number of long-term, trusted client relationships and was generating three million pounds' worth of revenue for his firm each year. Stephen was very good at his job.

However, when I first met Stephen he was bruised. He had just been through his firm's internal partner promotion process. Unfortunately, he hadn't made it. He wasn't on the cusp, it wasn't a near miss: it was a spectacular failure. The feedback was that Stephen just wasn't showing the leadership skills required to be perceived by the rest of the partnership as a fellow partner. During the course of the high-pressure assessment – involving the presentation of his business case, panel interviews, simulated client and team role-plays, and a group exercise looking at collaboration and the ability to grasp and articulate a new topic fast – Stephen did not inspire the decision-makers with confidence. The feedback was that he appeared nervous. He appeared under pressure. He was loquacious, and as a result, his messages were not clear. He couldn't engage others. He was dull. In short, he was not perceived as a leader, an ambassador of the firm.

A senior partner advised Stephen to defer. His view was

that the perception of Stephen's performance was so poor that it would be madness to try for promotion again straight away. He suggested that Stephen wait, and try again in two years' time. But Stephen wasn't prepared to wait. He was determined to move up to the next level as fast as he could. It was agreed that he could have some communication and impact coaching. We started to work together to develop Stephen's leadership skills and ensure that, next time, the decision-makers perceived him as senior, not junior; as a leader, not a follower.

Stephen describes himself as a nerd. He's a techie. He's an analyst. He's comfortable with numbers and figures. He is a natural introvert. When I first started working with Stephen, it was clear to me why he hadn't been promoted first time round. First impressions told me there was a lot to work on. As a subject-matter expert with huge knowledge of the detail, he had a tendency to talk without end, immediately diving into the weeds and losing his audience. Despite being tall and broad, which gave him a striking physical presence, when he was 'in the spotlight' there was a wooden quality and awkwardness in the way he carried himself. This conveyed the message that 'I'm not happy here, I'm feeling uncomfortable.'

This is the cruelty of perception. Over time, Stephen had established rock-solid credibility and built strong relationships with many clients who came back to him again and again for help with their problems. 'Give me six months with someone, and I'm fine,' he would quip. His sponsoring partners knew this. In fact, within his own business area and specialist sector he had a lot of backing from other partners in his case for partnership.

But it was the first impression, the immediate impact that

wasn't working. In an interview situation, in front of a group of strangers who are asking themselves, 'Is this person partner material?' the ability to have immediate impact and make a positive, confident first impression is essential.

So we had quite a lot of work to do, and not much time in which to do it. First, we started with Stephen's physicality: the message his body language was giving. Stephen worked hard on his posture, both standing and at the meeting table. It was critical that he started to 'own his space'. This was about finding a height and breadth about his person which sent the signal: 'I'm comfortable here. I deserve to be here.' This is always tough to do.

We never stoop, shrink or make ourselves physically smaller when we are young. We are blissfully unaware of ourselves. But as we grow up, we become more self-conscious. Often we are unaware that our bodies are sending out apologetic or timid signals. Stephen had to work hard to change his body language After all, his body had been carrying itself in this way for over thirty years. The default settings of his body and posture were programmed in.

The next thing we had to work on was bringing Stephen's messages and content to life. To be perceived as a leader, it is important to be able to communicate at a high level. To gain credibility as a possible partner, to get the buy-in, Stephen first had to be able to bring his past successes to life. Using the ingredients of story, I helped him to talk about his triumphs – how he had built client relationships, how he'd earned the trust of senior stakeholders and buyers, how he ensured that he and his team were indispensable to clients. It was important for Stephen to talk specifically rather than generally, to describe the little details and to add colour. For example, there is a huge difference between:

'There are three key areas I'd like to talk you through in relation to my business case. Number one: leveraging the firm.' *Snore.* I've switched off already. As opposed to:

'Let me tell you about how I build relationships with my clients and win work. I first met Andrew Worthington, COO at Alpha Asset Management, at a conference in Milan. As we started chatting I soon realized . . .' This is immediately engaging. It's the start of a story, based on Stephen's personal experience. The listener wants to know what happens next. Even better that the conclusion of this story is Stephen billing £1.5 million. Later, in the presentation of his business case, Stephen told another anecdote about how, when Michelle, one of his senior and trusted clients, moved from one business to another, it wasn't long before she called Stephen and asked him to pitch for a huge piece of work that she needed help with.

At first, Stephen wasn't comfortable speaking personally and using real names and real experiences. He challenged me all the way. 'This won't mean anything to them,' he argued. 'Why is it important that I use Andrew's name? Why do I have to talk about the numbers? They can read it on the slide.' But it's the specificity of personal experience that makes messages powerful. Rather than coming across as dull and conceptual, Stephen was coming across as engaging and memorable. The more he talked personally, the more confident and comfortable he appeared.

If you learn to play the piano, you have to practise. It feels unnatural and difficult. But over time, it starts to feel less difficult. You master the techniques required for your fingers to move nimbly and swiftly, to interpret the music easily, to add the musical dynamics. It can be a slog. You may think, *I hate music, why am I doing this? Why do I have to go over and over this piece in order to get it right?* But gradually the techniques and skills start to feel natural. They belong to you. You may start at Grade 1 and end up at Grade 8. By now you can play classical, jazz and blues. You can sight read with no practice. You can even enjoy improvising. Learning communication skills and becoming self-aware works exactly the same way.

One year later, Stephen went through the partner assessment process for a second time. He passed with flying colours. In a highly competitive field, he was in the top five per cent. A senior partner on the panel was heard to say, 'Why the heck didn't Stephen get through last time – that was an error of judgement on our part, wasn't it?' Stephen and I were both thrilled.

Stephen and I worked together to tackle a specific career hurdle. But Stephen has now integrated the coaching into his everyday business life. He can walk into any meeting without feeling nervous. He has the ability and awareness to come across as warm, personable and engaging, even if he is unprepared. He can comfortably build relationships with senior people and clients he doesn't know. He can contribute on topics which are not in his area of expertise. He can judge the right level of detail to use. He is never boring. He has learnt it all. He has practised, practised, practised. And all of these skills are now, very nearly, second nature to him. Over time, he will forget he learnt them at all.

7:

THE BIG SPEECH

Congratulations! You've been asked to give a Big Speech. Perhaps this is an important announcement you're giving to your whole company. It could be a speech to the partners of your firm ahead of a massive change. It could be a speech to your school, or university. It could be a conference speech. It could be a presentation to a small group of people on whom you are testing some ideas that you really believe in. You might be launching your book at a literature festival, or giving a TED talk. Whatever the format, this chapter is for you.

In a brilliant Big Speech the audience – digital or live – can be moved to a standing ovation or to tears. Or both. Yet Big Speeches can also come across as nervous and stilted, with content that doesn't quite ring true. I've watched speeches that surprised – either because the message haunted me for days afterwards, or because the message simply failed to land.

The speaker needs the skills to come across as engaging and compelling in the spotlight, and to lead and steer an intellectually powerful audience. They need to bring their messages to life and present themselves with gravitas and authority.

Sounds terrifying, right? One client who gave a TED talk spoke of the moment that he walked onto the red dot in the middle of the TED stage as the most frightening and exciting moment of his life. 'If people are giving a talk like it's a make or break for their lives, that's because it is. One thing you'll notice is that nobody's second talk is as good as their first. Standing on that red spot for the first time is like a bungee jump, and while some people keep chasing the dragon it takes a lot to recreate that first-time feeling.'

I've heard similar comments from a client who was launching her book at the Jaipur Literature Festival:

I'd given talks before but never to an audience anywhere near as big as Jaipur – the largest free literary festival on earth. With nearly a quarter of a million people over five days, even the smallest of the seven venues is guaranteed to pull an audience of hundreds. I remember walking about in a daze in the hours before my slot, wondering whether I should be trying to focus, remember what I had to say, or just chill out and risk forgetting everything. I knew there were going to be cameras filming me from the back of the tent and gigantic screens on either side of the stage projecting an image of me, talking, to the back of the room, and reviewers and bloggers in the audience. I'm not sure if it was helpful or not to have the familiar faces of my husband and friends looking up at me from the front row. In a sense, you become someone else in front of an audience like that. You have to perform, to expand yourself physically and mentally, and fill the place with what you're saying. I imagine it's somewhere close to being an actor.

The great news is that a good Big Speech is a specialized version of everything else I've been addressing in this book.

Why are you opening your mouth?

No matter how important you are, or think you are, the audience should be at the heart of your talk. The best speeches are tailored for the audience. Keep these questions in your mind as you are preparing:

- What facts do I want the audience to walk away with?
- How do I want them to feel at the end of the talk?
- What do I want them to do as a result of my speech?
- Why should the audience care about what I'm saying?

The audience

In my communication training experience I have still never come across anyone who has been asked to speak to the Borg. Non-Trekkies, bear with me. The Borg is a collection of alien creatures from the *Star Trek* series that have been assimilated by the collective, known as the Borg. Their individual experience is added to that of the group, so all thoughts and memories are the same. If you spoke to the Borg – as long as you had been assimilated by them – they'd understand what you were saying, no matter how many bits of jargon you threw in.

For anyone giving any big speech: think hard about the audience. Younger members won't have the experience of more seasoned members. People from Finance won't have the same background as those from HR. *Speak to all at the same time.*

How?

No jargon or acronyms

No specialized words that normal people can't understand. At Bloomberg, the shorthand for this was 'speak to dopes and pros' – at the same time. This was also referred to as speaking to both 'Aunt Edna worried about her pension, and the bond trader contemplating his next trade'. Or, as Albert Einstein put it, 'I speak to everyone in the same way, whether he is the garbage man or the president of the university.' My dad always said that you could tell if someone really knew their subject because they could explain it in words anyone could understand. And if you didn't get it the first time, they could explain it again.

For more, see the section on jargon in Chapter 3.

Are you being filmed?

If you are, and you're lucky (or in charge) you can get the video edited. All 'ums' and technical hitches magically vanish during the editing process, thanks to the multiple cameras trained on you at any time. If you stop to take a drink of water, this can be edited out. One client told me of a speaker on the stage before him who kept freezing while she gave her speech. The audience was encouraged to give her a huge clap as a vote of confidence, which allowed her to continue and finish. The speech ended up on the internet without any of the worrisome nervy bits.

If your Big Speech is being filmed, and you know it'll be edited, then this is a bonus. If you do make a mistake then it's worth having a word with the editor to make sure you're happy with how the mistake has been handled. It is rare to have the luxury of having someone else mop up after us, so make the most of it.

Props

I've seen some noteworthy props in TED talks. Jill Bolte Taylor used a human brain – complete with spinal cord – to illustrate her talk about having a stroke. For her own talk on the power of introverts, Susan Cain uses a suitcase full of old books that she brought to summer camp when she was little. The monk Andy Puddicome juggles with three oranges on stage to make the comparison between juggling and mindfulness.

Props can be useful for any presentation when used carefully. One fund manager I worked with wanted to spice up her presentation to clients. On a recent visit to a European car manufacturer she'd toured a factory run entirely by robots. She'd been so struck by the sight of efficiency and productivity that she snapped a photo on her phone. This photo proved to be incredibly useful in client presentations, as it described exactly why she had chosen to invest in this company's stock.

The speech by Mohammed Qahtani – the Saudi Arabian security engineer who won the 2015 title of Toastmasters International World Champion of Public Speaking – is a great example of the power of a prop.* Mohammed's speech, called 'The Power of Words', makes excellent use of humour, pauses and deeply personal anecdotes. But what sets it apart is Mohammed's opening, when he walks on stage and – before saying a word – flicks a lighter and starts to light a cigarette. There are a few gasps from the audience, and he responds by looking at them and asking, 'What?'

I saw Dominic Lawson speak during a debate on capitalism at the Names Not Numbers conference. He brought a couple of cans of baked beans to illustrate how capitalism works. He pointed out the trees cut down to make the paper

---

* See https://www.youtube.com/watch?v=qasE4ecA57Y.

label. The steel that makes the cans is both recycled and mined from iron ore. The farms that produce the beans are in the US and Canadian Great Lakes area. Meanwhile, the tomatoes travel to the factory from Spain and Portugal. To get the beans into the cans, the women who work in the factory put their kids into childcare. The crowning moment came when Lawson expressed his preference for the version of baked beans with pork sausages, which he offered up as 'cassoulet'.

Every time Brian Massey goes on stage, he wears a white lab coat and a pocket protector. His title is 'Conversion Scientist' – he works with companies to increase the number of sales they get from their websites. He is very aware of the risk this poses. He told me, 'I realize I can risk looking too gimmicky, and that I have to deliver a high-quality speech. But as long as I do, I'm just a little more memorable than the next guy.'*

Why do props work? They give the audience visual cues to remember. Those visuals will reside in the brain for longer than the words. Used sparingly, they are very powerful.

_____

* In fact, Massey's lab coat is not only a cue (or as Massey calls it, a 'peg' – namely, something a person can 'hang' impressions on for the audience to remember him), but also benefits from 'enclothed cognition' – the effect clothing has on cognitive processes. While wearing the scientific lab coat, Massey believes that he's a little bit cleverer than he actually is, and the audience perceives him to be cleverer as well.

Slides

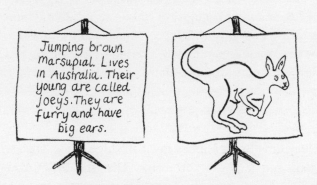

I am on the side of all who stand for eliminating 'death by PowerPoint'. Slides should be clear, precise and readable. There should never be too much information.

Whenever I'm asked to help a client design the slides for a presentation, the overriding message I give them is that **it is nearly impossible to read and listen at the same time.**

What you are doing is asking your brain to switch between listening and reading. While we like to delude ourselves that we're great at multitasking, neuroscience tells us that we aren't. We are moving from one task (listening) to another (reading, interpreting), and not everything is retained.

So if you are flooding someone with text and information on a slide, they can either listen to you or read the text. Not both.

Don't: read the information on the slide – DANGER! You'll lose the connection with the audience. They aren't making eye contact with you. You can't gauge your audience's attention or understanding.

Do, with care: put some text up on a slide and ask people to read it while you just stand next to it, silent. This can work, but your timing has to be perfect. It also doesn't really work in terms of impact, unless the information is so interesting/funny/astonishing that it speaks for itself.

One successful example that I saw recently was in a presentation by Campaign PR gurus Michael Hayman and Nick Giles. At the close of his presentation for their book, Michael put up a slide and let it speak for itself.

What we know about the brain backs this up.

Professor Olivier Oullier told me about his field work in retail stores and conference venues, in which he examines the difference between people 'watching' and people 'paying attention'. Using portable brain sensors and eye-tracking devices, he's monitored speakers using slides. If the audience have to look at the screen for too long they end up losing track of what the speaker is saying. Personally, he delivers his 'explanations' with a blank screen behind him so that they focus on his words, without any visual interference. He even cues the audience further by taking off his glasses when he's delivering an important point. He does so sparingly – only two or three times in a speech – to signal to the audience 'this is what you need to remember'.

As a rule, the audience should be able to take in the message of the slide within three seconds so that their attention can then be returned to the speaker. This holds true for any speech, big or small.

Each slide should only have one key message

Slides often have a life after the live performance. If your talk is filmed, it will be re-watched by people on their computers, tablets or phones. The latter is the most important: every slide has to be visible on your mobile.

This is great advice for everyone. Remember the times you've squinted into your phone as you try to enlarge important parts of a presentation? Imagine that this is *your* presentation and that your client has just decided not to bother. Why would you risk that happening?

Font choice

To be safe, go for sans serif fonts rather than serif fonts. In normal language, this means ones with clear, defined lines rather than ones with curly bits. Think Helvetica rather than Times New Roman.

Fonts which are good for slides:

Arial
Avenir
Calibri
Helvetica
Verdana

Fonts which are not great for slides:

Baskerville

Bookman

Bradley Hand

Times New Roman

Palatino

I am not saying that there is never a place for 'interesting' fonts. But they should be used sparingly.

Font size

Given the rule that your slides should be readable on the smallest iPhone screen, the text should be large enough to see comfortably on your handset.

Here's why – look how tiny the font gets on a phone.

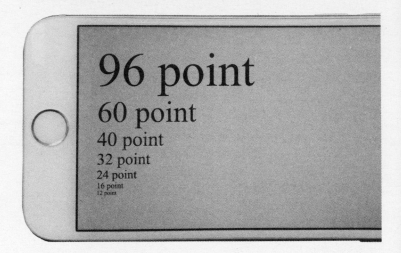

So the rule is, make the fonts as BIG as possible. The minimum font size is 24.

Pictures

We process visual information more efficiently than text. Reading is a skill we must learn, whereas the ability to process pictures is something we've been born with. So images make the audience connect with you quicker. They make your content easier to digest.

Consider the following two images. Both get the same point across, but the second does it faster and more intuitively.

If there is a picture that helps to tell the story – that adds something and doesn't distract from the narrative – then include it.

We know the brain has long- and short-term memory. Words are processed by the short-term memory. We can only keep about seven separate items at a time there. Images, however, go into long-term memory, and as most people are visual learners, using images will help underscore your messages in a way that will remain with them after your talk has finished.

There's also a digital reason for images. After a big speech, your slides will be seen on people's computers, tablets and phones. The smallest screen size dictates what you should have on your slide. Images often do tell a story better than words, sometimes even a thousand times over.

Colours on slides

Use contrasting colours on your slides, with the slide background as light or dark as possible, so that more colours will contrast against it. Blending mid-tone colours doesn't work so well.

Stick to your allotted time

Don't go over time. It's rude and unforgiveable. You are cutting into either the next speaker's time or the audience's. Rehearse to get the timing just right. I attended a conference at the European Parliament where speakers going overtime were drowned out by Beethoven's Ninth Symphony. Effective.

Summary

Think about your audience. They aren't clones of each other. They have different levels of experience and education. Think about what facts you want them to walk away with, how you want them to feel and what you want them to do as a result of your speech.

Speak to all of them at once, using words that intelligent teenagers could understand. Drop the management jargon, the acronyms and any specialist language that might get lost.

Consider using a prop – they work because they give the

audience visual cues to remember. Those visuals will reside in the brain for longer than the words. Used *sparingly*, they are very powerful.

Your slides matter. It is nearly impossible to read and listen at the same time. Keep one point per slide. Keep the fonts as large as possible (24 point is the smallest that is easily read on a phone) and think about the colour contrast on your slides. Use images. Our brain processes them much faster than it does text. When wrapping up, put a blank slide up.

Keep to the time you've been allotted. It's the most precious commodity we have. You'll lose the goodwill of the audience and the conference organizers if you go over. For a TED talk, you'll be cut off.

8:

THE BODY IS WIRED FOR IMAGES

This chapter tells you why well-crafted visuals work. Spoiler alert: they get you remembered and make people like you more!

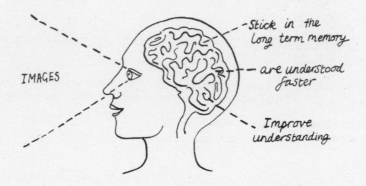

IMAGES

- Stick in the long term memory
- are understood faster
- Improve understanding

Professor Olivier Oullier pointed out to me that optical nerves are one of the first things to develop in a baby's brain as it starts to form. Everything related to the visual is the first to develop.

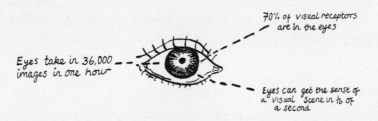

70% of visual receptors are in the eyes

Eyes take in 36,000 images in one hour

Eyes can get the sense of a visual scene in ⅒ of a second

This hints at the importance behind cueing the brain with visual words and pictures. They give associations which make the memory start to work. One of the easiest ways to help your audience keep what you say in their long-term memories is to pair ideas with relevant images.

It is perhaps no surprise that many people are classed as 'visual' learners.

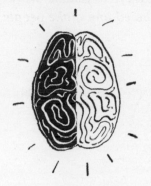

50% of the brain is used in visual processing

65% of us are visual learners

40% of nerve endings are linked to the retina

Pictures get you remembered

Edgar Dale was a professor at Ohio State University. His research on how people learn showed that the best way of learning is through a combination of reading, listening and experience. Check out what he learned about the recall of people listening to illustrated lectures.*

---

* Edgar Dale, *Audiovisual Methods in Teaching*, Dryden Press, 1969.

Presentation	Ability to Recall	
	after 3 hours	after 3 days
Spoken lecture	25 per cent	10–20 per cent
Written (reading)	72 per cent	10 per cent
Visual and verbal (illustrated lecture)	80 per cent	65 per cent

This is important! If you give a talk using only words, after three days your audience may remember just 10 per cent of what you say. However, if you use visuals while you speak, **they will remember 65 per cent of what you say**.

Pictures cut your meeting time

Using visuals cuts the amount of time you need to spend convincing people of your point of view. Who wants to lengthen the time they spend in meetings? Not me. Visuals help people to make decisions more quickly.

Robert Horn, visiting professor at Stanford University, used studies from, amongst other places, the Wharton School of Business to come up with some stunning findings.

He found that just using an overview map for your talk can help people to better organize and process information, and to act on it more promptly. In one study, 64 per cent of participants made an immediate decision following presentations that used an overview map.

What is an overview map? The more recent term is 'infographic' – a picture that explains a concept or idea. There's one coming up on page 112.

Robert Horn's research showed that visual language has been shown to shorten meetings by 24 per cent. Groups using visuals 'experienced a 21 per cent increase in their ability to reach consensus' compared to those who didn't.[*]

Visuals make people like you more

There is a fascinating study, conducted by Sebastian Kernbach, Martin J. Eppler and Sabrina Bresciani, called 'Use of Visualization in the Communication of Business Strategies: An Experimental Evaluation'. Behind the academic title lies some interesting research. The study tested whether using pictures to communicate a seven-minute business strategy was superior to using bullet-pointed lists of text. The presentation was for the financial services branch of an international car manufacturer, and involved real managers working for a real motor firm. One group was shown a block of text and the other two groups were shown more visual/graphic versions of the strategy.

The experiment found that those who were exposed to a graphic version of the strategy rather than the bullet points paid more attention, were more likely to endorse the strategy, and better recalled the strategy after an hour of working on an unrelated case study. Not only that, but managers who saw the visual versions *perceived the presenter in a significantly more positive light* than those who had seen the text strategy.[†]

---

[*] Robert E. Horn, *Visual Language: Global Communication for the 21st Century*, 1998.

[†] S. Kernbach, M. J. Eppler and S. Bresciani (2014), 'The Use of

Major goal: 7,5 million contracts

- Triple profit in diversified business
  - Establish service offerings for individual mobility
  - Innovate insurance solutions to significantly increase contribution
  - Introduce banking in defined markets

- Sustain profitable growth in mature business areas
  - Increase customer retention
  - Establish a unique understanding of the customer to sell more products
  - Provide high quality services and manage customer relationships

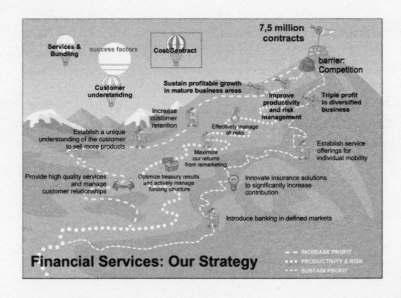

The slides in the study described above are still a little busy. Ideally, I would have broken them down even further, to one message per slide. But they are vastly better than the text.

Will it take more time to come up with compelling visuals for your talk? Yes. Is it worth it? Yes.

Summary

Optic nerves are the first things to develop in a baby's brain as it starts to form. We are programmed to receive visual images. Make use of this! Cue the brain with visual words and pictures. They give associations which make the memory start to work. Pair your messages with relevant images.

Scientists have shown that using illustrations in lectures gets your messages remembered for longer. They help people reach consensus and make decisions faster. Pictures cut your meeting time, and because they help the audience understand what the speaker is saying, the audience also views the presenter more positively.

A word of caution: we are sophisticated beings and are increasingly exposed to professional images and presentations. It isn't enough to throw a few images into your presentation. They need to be thought through. Remember, the brain needs to be surprised in order to pay attention.

Visualization in the Communication of Business Strategies: An Experimental Evaluation', *International Journal of Business Communication*, 52 (2): 164–87.

9:

CASE STUDY: THE BIG SPEECH

Clive was a senior banker at an international investment bank. He was COO. He was well liked and well respected both by his team and his senior stakeholders. He'd been around for a long time. Everyone thought he did a great job. But Clive had a ghastly secret: he hated speaking to large groups of people. He was absolutely terrified.

Clive was so scared of being on stage, in the spotlight, that he would do anything to avoid it. He became highly skilled at sidestepping, avoidance tactics, telling little white lies. To avoid one particular speaking engagement, he even went as far as to arrange to be out of the country!

When I first met Clive he admitted that he could no longer avoid public speaking. The seniority and profile of his role meant that it was no longer possible to sidestep. In fact, his inability to raise his profile and take the spotlight was beginning to become career-limiting. So we started to do some coaching work together. I started with some introductory communication and personal impact work to raise Clive's self-awareness and self-confidence. The next stage was to help Clive prepare for an important, high-profile speaking engagement at a conference in the States. Needless to say, Clive was dreading this.

Clive was an immensely likeable fellow. I warmed to him straight away. It was easy to tell that he was dependable, solid and a safe pair of hands. If Clive said he would do something, you knew instinctively it would get done. And it would be well done. He was pro-active at developing and supporting his team. People really enjoyed working for him.

However, in the spotlight I saw a very different version of Clive. He seemed to physically shrink. His face became ashen grey; in fact, he looked much older. His voice was quiet. He swallowed his words. The whole impression was one of timidity. He looked and sounded like a junior member of staff, not like a senior leader. And it was dull. If he was going to ski down the black run, I'm afraid to say it wouldn't be long before Clive was spread-eagled, face first in the snow.

First stop: energy. Clive found injecting energy into his communication style hard. He was cerebral, not physical. But he really liked what energy did for him. The addition to Clive's style of vocal and physical energy completely changed our perception of him. He grew physically in stature and started to have presence. It looked like he owned the stage rather than the stage owning him. The addition of vocal energy techniques gave his voice colour, music and warmth. His face transformed from looking worried and, at times, downright miserable, to being smiley and positive. The extraordinary thing was that he looked ten years younger. Clive was delighted with this! I love this aspect of energy. Dynamic energy levels can make you blossom and bloom in so many unexpected ways.

Next stop: content. Clive had a tendency to talk in lists and jargon. I often challenged him: 'OK, Clive, if you were at home, sitting at your kitchen table, how would you com-municate this idea to your wife and children? You wouldn't say "geographies". You'd say "countries". You wouldn't say "bandwidth". You'd say "time".'

Clive admitted, 'My wife would think I was a freak if I used this language at home. I think she'd divorce me!'

We had some heated debates. 'Surely I can't say it like that. I sound completely unprofessional.'

To which I'd reply, 'But if you say it your way, Clive, you sound like a robot. I stopped listening ages ago and was thinking about what I wanted for supper.'

We worked hard to find the appropriate stories, examples and anecdotes to illustrate the points Clive wanted to make. He had had a long and illustrious career and was a very experienced banker with a lot of experience to draw on. This was fantastic. In the end we had too much material, and plenty ended up on the cutting room floor.

Clive set off for the States with a spring in his step. He felt rehearsed and prepared. He was ready to tackle the black run. He rang me after the event. He was delighted. He had never received such positive feedback. He had been thumped on the back. His hand had nearly fallen off – it had never been shaken so many times in quick succession. In the following days, he received over forty emails of congratulations. This was very different to the complete lack of feedback he had received in the past – because no one knew quite what to say. Clive even admitted that he had volunteered to speak at another conference in Canada a few months later.

Clive and I continued to do work together. It was very exciting. He got to the point that I believe everyone can get to with practice and self-belief. Instead of having a week of sleepless nights before a big event, Clive began to look forward to giving speeches. Even better – thanks to technique, and lots of it – not only could Clive now tackle the black runs with relative ease, he even had the confidence to go off-piste, improvising and ad-libbing when it was appropriate. He now had confidence, skill and self-awareness. Clive began to get a buzz from performing. Bingo.

A few more dos and don'ts

Do: prepare your own speech. I know it's tempting to get your internal communications team to write it for you, but this puts you in a stressful position. The language and ideas are not your own, and it becomes much harder to connect emotionally to your content. Danger – you appear disengaged and inauthentic.

Do: spend a few moments on stage, taking the audience in, before you start to speak. However nervous you are feeling, this will give the impression that you are calm, confident and in control.

Do: share your eye contact around the room. When you are nervous, it is tempting to pick a friendly face in the audience and only talk to them. Danger – this tells the rest of the audience that you are unconfident. An analogy for good eye contact is to imagine that you are handing out sweets individually rather than chucking them out by the fistful. Everyone in the auditorium gets a sweet. This means making eye contact with everyone in the room (or, for large audiences, every section of the auditorium) and holding it for a few seconds before moving to the next person/section.

Do: name-check people in the audience, even if there are 500 people in the room. This can help create an informal, personable atmosphere in what can be a formal, stultifying environment. Sometimes a client will say to me, 'But surely

I can't name-check one person and leave everyone else out? It will be perceived as favouritism.' Of course, it's impossible to name-check everyone in the audience. If you are worried, try saying, 'I'm sorry to say I can't talk about every success that every partner has had this year, but to give one example . . .' Your audience will understand this.

Don't: make unconscious movements. It's easy to sway, drift or fidget without being aware of it. On a stage or in front of a large group of people, this is incredibly distracting. Danger – if we are noticing that the speaker is swaying to and fro, it means that we are *not listening* to what you are saying. Plant the feet solidly, hip-width apart and stay rooted. From this position all of your energy can be transmitted to your audience with your voice, hands and face. Your movement should be conscious, not unconscious.

Do: keep asking yourself, 'What slides can I cut?' You are far more interesting than a slide. We never need slides to communicate our social lives.

Don't: talk to the slides. Talk to the audience.

Don't: get trapped behind a lectern. A lectern is a comfort blanket. Our notes will be on the lectern and our tendency is to become surgically attached to them. Danger – this looks like we are nervous or don't know our stuff. If we are trapped behind a lectern, our energy, dynamism and personality is trapped too. Be brave. Come out into the middle of the room or stage, and own the space. Leave your notes on a table nearby so they are there to support you if you need them.

Don't: rely on the slides to prompt you. Danger – you start to sound like a written document. Dull, dull, dull. Your own hand-prepared notes should give you prompts and triggers to help you talk conversationally and use story and examples.

Don't: rely on a microphone to provide your vocal energy. The microphone magnifies what you give it. So, if you are speaking in a monotone with no pause, the microphone will project a monotone with no pause.

Don't: be tempted to busk it. I can't tell you how many times clients have told me that they prefer not to rehearse because, on one occasion, when they didn't rehearse, it went really well and felt natural and spontaneous. Danger – this is a fluke. This happens one in a hundred times! You wouldn't risk sitting an exam without revising. Practice makes perfect!

Do: try and enjoy it. Maybe this sounds absurd. But remember: as we learned in Chapter 2, the audience mirrors us. If we look like we are pleased to be there, the audience will feel the same.

10:

HOW TO START – AND END – STRONG

Having trouble getting started? Or figuring out how to knock it out of the park at the end? This chapter is for you. Plus, a note on how to deal with nerves.

How to start – the beginning of a speech. Or a big meeting. Or a job interview. The nerves can be firing. The palms can be sweating. Regardless of whether it's a board presentation, a TED talk or a promotion panel, the first few seconds are tough. Often my clients tell me, 'After the first two minutes I'm OK, I'm into the flow.'

Unfortunately, no one in a meeting gives you two minutes to warm up. No one would expect a concert pianist to arrive on stage, then sit down and work through a few scales and arpeggios before getting cracking with the sonata.

The first minutes are critically important, because human beings are quick to judge.

There is a concept in psychology called 'anchoring'. It refers to the tendency of humans to 'anchor', or rely too

heavily, on one trait or piece of information when making decisions. If you start poorly there's a good chance they'll 'anchor' or focus on that, making them less likely to buy into you and harder for you to get back on track.

There's been a great deal written about 'rapid cognition' – the first two seconds of impressions when interviewing someone for a job, or seeing someone on a street. Malcolm Gladwell's book *Blink* is an eye-opener on this subject. These snap judgements are sometimes useful, but they can also have darker sides. Think of racial or sexual discrimination based on the way someone appears. Our ability to 'thin-slice', or make observations, impressions and judgements about people, is part of what makes us human.[*]

So we have a couple of seconds to grab and hold someone's attention. How do you do it?

A great way to begin is – simply – not to begin. In a speech, come on stage . . . and then stop. Pause. Look around. Gauge the audience. This will give you valuable information about the state they're in. Are they hungry,

---

[*] Malcolm Gladwell, *Blink: The Power of Thinking Without Thinking* (2005).

attentive, bored, fidgety? This pause will also give the impression of gravitas. In the video of Leonard Bernstein's famous 1973 'The Unanswered Question' Norton lecture at Harvard, he waits a full nine seconds before starting to speak. These are still some of the most highly regarded lectures on music.

The hook!

Think of Beethoven's famous Fifth Symphony. Its first notes are known as 'the famous four notes': *Da Da Da DAAAAAA*. They are simple, loud, have cadence, rhythm and (you guessed it) start with a pause. Then there's another pause. The beginning of your speech should be just as cracking. This is not to say that you need to shout at the audience. But by getting the energy up at the start, you show them how you mean to continue, where you'll come back to, what the theme will be. Professor Olivier Oullier thinks Beethoven knew that after a few minutes, the audience would fall asleep. The 'punches', as he calls them, serve to 'wake the audience up'.

Right from the start, you have to hook the audience. Emotion is always a cracking way to hook them. 'I'm delighted to be here.' 'I'm really looking forward to speaking to you about . . .' 'I'm passionate about . . .'

As a neuroscientist, Oullier is keenly aware that if you

don't surprise people right at the start, you risk losing them. He sets up his speeches by telling the audience that he has a 'special take' on the subject matter. So if he is giving a speech about his work on the brain, diet and nutrition, he'll start out by setting himself up as the expert – not just with lab work but also by collecting data about people's behaviour in their real lives. Everyone thinks they know a lot about diet and nutrition, so you have to surprise the audience by giving them a reason to stay tuned. 'I'm going to tell you something you'll be incredibly surprised to hear.' 'Let me tell you about my unique approach to . . .'

This way, the audience will anchor to the 'special take' (on diet and nutrition) rather than just 'diet and nutrition'.

As Oullier puts it, 'start with the unique feature that makes your knowledge special. This determines whether people will stay with you through the opening, or groan and think, "oh yeah I know this already".'

Another way to start the speech, says Oullier, is to 'ask the question that only you can answer'.

A great way to start if your audience doesn't know you particularly well is to introduce yourself. I've seen this done incredibly cleverly. Octavius Black, the CEO of MindGym, a company that teaches businesses how to use psychology to get better results, introduced himself this way:

> *I didn't start off life as Octavius. I actually started out as Orlando. One day when I was about five, my mother asked my father what he'd like to do that day. He said, 'Why don't we change the kid's name today?' My mum was sewing O. Black name tags onto my clothes at the time so she said, 'You can have any name as long as it starts with O.' My father said, 'How about Octavius or*

*Oedipus?' It's perhaps that beginning that got me
interested in psychology.**

A word on nerves

Nerves are a killer. I'd love to wave the magic wand and
make them go away. Yet they are part of life. The actor
Laurence Olivier is quoted as saying, 'If you're not nervous,
you're dead.' There's a neuro-linguistic programming
technique used by Lucian Tarnowski, founder and CEO of
BraveNew.com, that I like as it is both practical and portable. You need to set yourself up for it ahead of time.

Here's how he describes it. Find a time and place when
you are really relaxed at home. Close your eyes. Imagine
your favourite place on the planet. Somewhere you have
been before without a worry in the world. Perhaps your
favourite beach. Imagine your partner or best friend lying
next to you. Your favourite drink by your side. Feel the sun
on your skin. Hear the sound of the waves (or whatever
sounds accompany your favourite place). Try to picture
every little detail – the colour of the water, the texture of the
sand, the feeling of being completely relaxed and sublime.
Really focus on this and take it all in. Smile.

Then with your right hand stroke a knuckle on your left
hand. I like to stroke my middle finger with my index finger.
What you are doing is creating a mental association with the
feeling of stroking your knuckle. Since this is a very particular feeling, your body can remember it. Practise this a few

_____

* I heard Octavius Black speak at the Names Not Numbers conference
in London in 2016.

times in a relaxed place. Now, when you are about to go up and speak, stroke your knuckle (close your eyes if you need to). Your mind will bring back the image of your favourite place. This will distract you from the nervousness you will be feeling about speaking. It will lower your heart rate and allow you to take a deep breath and collect yourself. Let out that deep breath with a smile and know that you are ready to share yourself with the people you are speaking to. Go and hit it out of the park.

If your nerves get the better of you at any point while you are speaking, just pause, take a breath and stroke your knuckle and then carry on again.

End strong

My children's piano teacher tells them, when they are preparing for an exam, to be sure to end their piece 'strong'. They practise the ending over and over to make sure that, even if there has been a slip-up in the middle somewhere, the examiner will hear the closing bars performed with the expression, dynamics and articulation that the composer intended.

Your closing remarks are equally vital. Plan them word for word. If you've created a great impression from the beginning of the speech, you want to continue this right until the end.

Here are a few ways to close a presentation or a speech.

— Tell a personal story that illustrates your message.

— Find a quotation that illustrates your point. If it is well known, add your own twist to the quotation.

— If you are using slides, leave a quotation, a striking picture or a cartoon on the screen. Current references are often less 'tired' than familiar ones. Keep surprising the audience.

— End with a call to action. Think of politicians encouraging the audience to get out of their armchairs and vote. Give them something to go and do. In Ron Finley's TED talk on planting vegetables in abandoned lots of land in South Central LA, he finishes by saying, 'So basically, if you want to meet with me, you know, if you want to meet, don't call me if you want to sit around in cushy chairs and have meetings where you talk about doing some shit – where you *talk* about doing some shit. If you want to meet with me, come to the garden with your shovel so we can plant some shit.' He gets a standing ovation.[*]

— Inspire your audience with hope.

— Bring out a prop.

— Find your own memorable soundbite to leave the audience with. (Think of 'Stay hungry, stay foolish' by Steve Jobs in his Stanford commencement address. He actually took these from the back of the Whole Earth catalogue. Inspiration can come from anywhere.)

— Think of three words that underscore your message. Alan Siegel finishes his TED talk on simplifying legal language by saying, 'How are we going to change the

---

[*]   Ron Finley, TED 2013. See https://www.ted.com/talks/ron_finley_a_guerilla_gardener_in_south_central_la?language=en.

world? Make clarity, transparency and simplicity a national priority.'*

— Finish with a surprising fact. Keep challenging your audience.

— Your ending needs to bring your message home. In a recent children's music recital where the kids were judged by a professional musician, the adjudicator finished his comments to the assembled six-to-ten-year-olds and their parents by saying, 'Never let the good be the enemy of the better.' We all know the message (keep practising), but somehow this elevated the message for me.

All of the 'energy' techniques I've spoken about will help you do this. With pauses, moving your voice around, emphasis and volume, signal to the audience that you're wrapping it up. If you are using slides, have a blank screen behind you at the end.

If you are taking questions, think how to signal that.

Don't say: 'Um, that's it. Any questions?'

Don't say: 'Sorry to go on for so long. I know it can be boring.'

Do say: 'I'll take questions in a moment, but before I do, I want to leave you with this story.' Then tell the story.

Then, once you're finished, just be finished. Resist the temptation to organize your notes, fiddle with your clothes

---

* Alan Siegel, TED2010. See https://www.ted.com/talks/alan_siegel_let_s_simplify_legal_jargon?language=en.

or do anything that signals nerves. Then just hold the silence. If people are going to clap, usually they won't all start at once. One person will start. Look at that person and say thank you. Then as more start to clap, look at the next person and say thank you.

In a smaller presentation, when clapping isn't going to happen, then do the same. Stay focused. Smile and just wait.

It will increase your gravitas and the trust that the audience puts in you.

Summary

Plan the beginning of a speech, or your opening line in a meeting. Human beings are programmed to make quick judgements and are prone to anchoring their lasting impressions on their first take of you.

Pause before you begin. Consider introducing yourself with a story that connects you to your subject. Hook the audience with dynamic energy, with emotion, and highlight your unique approach to the subject you're going to be talking about.

End strong. Tell a personal story, or leave the audience with a powerful quotation. If you want to motivate the audience to do something, then end with a call to action. Bring your message home with a prop.

When you're done, be done. Don't trail off. Hold the silence at the end with eye contact. Don't fiddle with papers or clothes. Wait for the questions or clapping.

11:

CASE STUDY: PITCHING FOR BUSINESS

It's a competitive world out there. One city law firm can offer much the same as another city law firm. One professional services firm can offer a pretty much identical service to the next professional services firm. One investment bank is much the same as the bank next door. Sorry, but from the client's perspective, it's true. There might be a difference in price. There might be a difference in timescales. But there is little difference in expertise, brain power or the ability to get the job done.

So what is the differentiating factor? I have worked with many businesses over the years as the leadership struggle to identify and communicate their Unique Selling Point. What is it about our business that makes us different? Why should graduates want to come and work for our firm rather than for our competitors? Why is our business the best?

Of course, there are differentiators. One asset manager may invest in Japan but not China. One law firm might have offices in the Middle East, not South America. But for me, the most important differentiator is the people. What is a business without its people? It is the people who make the business unique and ultimately successful.

This is why we pitch, whether formally or informally, for work. Human beings want to work with other human beings – people they like and trust, and with whom they can build a relationship,

We're all pitching all the time. On a first date, we're pitching ourselves. Meeting a new group of potential friends at university, we're pitching ourselves. Performers and actors pitch all the time. There are dozens of actors who are capable of giving a fantastic performance as Lady Macbeth, but any sensible director holds an audition process. Not only does the director have to discover whether an actress can handle Shakespeare's iambic pentameter and has sufficient emotional range for the part, but the director is also asking 'Can I work with this person?' 'Are they going to get on with the other actors?' 'Are they confident and do they have stamina?' 'Is there chemistry between my two leads?'

The political process might seem easier if potential MPs were able to win our votes by posting their CVs and personal statements through our letter boxes – but a CV doesn't tell us enough. A CV doesn't really tell us anything. This is why there are political hustings, rallies, TV debates – we need to see the whites of the candidate's eyes. In the polling booth we give our vote to the politician who is credible, who we feel an affinity with, who we believe can negotiate on our behalf.

Likewise, if we're trying to win business from a new

client, we don't put our company literature in the post, send a few emails, cross our fingers and hope we get the work. The potential client needs to meet us and see if there is a mutual chemistry. If there's a tough deadline which involves working through the night, are you the team the client wants to share a pizza with? You know how dogs sniff each other when they meet on street corners – it's much the same.

I was recently helping a team of consultants prepare to pitch to a high-profile, UK-based engineering firm. I had received a last-minute call from Emma, the project leader, who realized that this opportunity was too big to miss and that the team needed to do everything possible to give themselves the best opportunity to win. This piece of work was going to be worth approximately £8 million over three to four years.

When I arrived on Monday morning, there was tension in the air. The 'verbals', i.e. the face-to-face meeting, was in forty-eight hours, and, as is so often the case, 90 per cent of the preparation thus far had been in preparing the written documents and the slide pack. Not one of the three presenters had begun to prepare for the forty-minute 'presentation', or the thirty minutes of questions and answers.

Now, I am not for one moment suggesting that the written documents aren't important. Of course they are. But spending 90 per cent of the preparation time on the written side of things and 10 per cent of the time on the verbal piece is a bit like preparing to run a marathon by eating healthily for a couple of weeks and buying all the sports kit – the snazziest trainers, the latest Lycra – before realizing, on the morning of the race, 'Oh no! I haven't done any training!'

Time was short. So, to see where we were, I gave everyone the opportunity to prepare their content and messages and then, with the help of my camera, asked them to have a first bash at what they might want to convey to the client the next day.

Oh dear.

Martin, the most senior member of the team, the man who was topping and tailing the presentation, came across as nervous and bland. Andy, the subject-matter expert, was long-winded, too technical and had a tendency to dazzle us with incomprehensible jargon. Liz, the would-be day-to-day project manager and the main point of contact for the client, fared slightly better. She had the beginnings of some energy and warmth and a conversational style which made her immediately more compelling. But she was speaking at 100 mph.

When everyone had finished, Emma and I realized that neither of us could remember a word anyone had said. No messages had landed whatsoever.

What I've observed over many years of working with individuals and pitch teams is that when we pitch, it often becomes all about 'us': who we are, where we're based, how many of us there are in the office, our global reach, why we're a premier firm, etc. **But why is this interesting or relevant for the client?** My answer? It's not.

Everything you say has to be said for a reason. It is vital to ask yourself – what is my message here? Why am I saying this? What is the benefit for the client? Why is it relevant for them? It is vital that you put yourself in your client's shoes and ask, so what? I call it the 'So what?' factor.

Martin, Andy, Liz and I went back to the drawing board. I started to help them prepare their content from the perspective of the client. Our starting point was to ask some questions.

- What is the client trying to achieve?
- What is the client's vision?
- What is the client worried about?
- What pressures is the client currently facing?
- What do we know about the client – how do they like to work?

Only when we had answered these questions, from the client as a whole and from the perspective of each individual stakeholder on the client panel, could we begin to work out what Martin, Andy and Liz needed to say.

You may be thinking: well, this is all obvious stuff. Completely obvious. But too often, we don't do it.

The next step was to decide which specific examples, stories and personal anecdotes Martin, Andy and Liz could tell to convince the panel that they had bags of experience, and had worked on similar projects in the past for which they had received glowing client feedback. Martin began to talk about the experience of his team members, selling them in glowing terms by illustrating their past successes. Andy stopped 'transmitting' and started to talk simply and with humour about complex and technical ideas, using analogy and metaphor to great effect. Liz told a fantastic story about a similar project she had managed the previous year, when she and her team had beaten the client's deadline by five days. As a result, the confidence, status and likeability factor went up tenfold. Everything was tailored, everything was specific, everything was relevant.

Martin, Andy and Liz became interesting and compelling. What they said had a point. A lot of positive messages landed. They got the job.

Pitches: dos and don'ts

Do: devote equal time to preparing the written content and rehearsing the verbal content.

Do: keep ruthlessly culling your slides. Keep asking yourself – do I really need that one? When you are telling a relevant story based on your personal experience, you are selling yourself far more effectively than any graph can do.

Don't: stuff your slides with too much information. We just can't take it in. Keep them simple.

Do: use images whenever you can on your slides.

Do: divide the talking equally. If the most senior person in the room barely speaks and the most junior person in the room speaks all the time (because they're the best at talking), your client is getting a mixed message. What is the point of this senior person? In addition, a variety of different people and different voices helps keep the panel engaged.

Don't: look bored or fall asleep when a fellow team member is talking. It happens! It's important to listen actively, listen with energy, nodding or even, on occasion, verbalizing a thought: 'yes, absolutely'.

Don't: be afraid to interject during your team member's presentation, e.g. 'Can I just leap in there, Rachel, and mention something . . .' This helps you appear cohesive and tight-knit. The perception is that you work well together and are confident enough to pass the baton between you. It adds a level of surprise and spontaneity to the meeting. If you are nervous about this, it can be helpful to plan these 'spontaneous' interjections.

Do: use names. Refer to the names of people in your team and use the names of the individual panel members. This can help make a high-pressure or formal situation feel more conversational and informal.

Do: keep upping the energy. Pass the baton to your team member with plenty of vocal energy. Likewise, when you're taking the baton, come in with more vocal and physical energy than the previous speaker. You don't want the panel to fall asleep.

Do: encourage questions and interaction along the way. The more interactive it is, the more engaged the panel will be.

Don't: go over the allotted time. If you have been asked to speak for thirty minutes, my recommendation is that you prepare twenty minutes of material. Due to nerves and pressure, we tend to become more long-winded on the day. Less is more. It's important to get interactive as soon as you can.

Questions and answers: dos and don'ts

In my experience there are two camps. There are the people who find Q&A much easier than presenting because it feels more conversational and natural. The other group dread Q&A for fear of looking and sounding stupid – being caught off guard and being asked questions they haven't got an answer for.

Don't: start to answer straight away. This inevitably means that you are talking and thinking at the same time, which means that neither is as effective as it could be. The danger is that you become long-winded and repetitive. The second danger is that because you are giving yourself no time to consider your answer, it is easy to appear rushed and under pressure.

Don't: let your energy drop during Q&A. The questioner might have very low vocal and physical energy. Our natural tendency is to mimic and match. The danger here is that the energy in the room drops and that you start to be perceived as less sure-footed and authoritative.

Don't: all have a go at answering the same question. In a team Q&A session, it's tempting to think 'I don't think my colleague has answered that well' or 'I'd like to add something to that.' Suddenly three people have all answered the same question, your team have been talking for fifteen minutes and the panel are thinking, 'will they ever shut up?'

Do: pause. As soon as the question has been asked – pause. You need time to think and clarify your thoughts.

Do: acknowledge the question. A great way to do this is to repeat or paraphrase the question, just as you might do in a job interview – so, for example, 'Why are you more expensive than your competitors?' could be met with 'OK, so you're asking, why are we more expensive than our competitors?' Pause. 'Well, the reason for that is . . .' This is a fantastic technique because it allows the questioner to feel heard and understood. It also buys you plenty of time to clarify the question and think, OK, what's the best way for me to answer this? The time and space you give yourself using this technique heightens your authority and confidence.

Do: respond with variations on 'That's a good question,' or 'I thought you might ask me that question,' or 'That's an interesting question,' or even, 'I'm so glad you asked me that question.' This suggests that you are pleased to answer any question; indeed, you are relishing them, rather than thinking, 'oh God, I really hope they don't ask me that one . . .'

Do: ask questions back. This is important. Lots of people ask unclear or poorly articulated questions. It's vital to clarify what it is they want to know, or, if you are uncertain, why the questioner is asking that particular question. It is dangerous to attempt to answer a vague or badly worded question. Inevitably your response will be vague and badly worded.

Do: check in with the questioner. It's important for you to know that they are 'with you' and not confused or unclear. Useful comebacks are 'Does that answer your question?' and 'Is there anything else you'd like me to talk about on that point?' By checking in and asking questions back, you are taking the reins of the interaction. You are no longer a passenger or an interviewee. It is no longer the 'buyer' with the status and the 'seller' remaining impotent. Now you are driving and steering the meeting. It starts to feel like a conversation between two equals, rather than a question and answer session.

Do: when they are answering a question, look at your fellow team member as if they're the most charismatic and attractive person you have ever seen. Your ability to give them attention and focus encourages the rest of the room to give them attention and focus.

Do: decide beforehand who is going to answer what. Your team will come across as cohesive and prepared.

Do: direct your answer to the whole panel, rather than only the questioner. It's important that everyone on the other side of the table feels engaged and included throughout.

Do: answer questions using examples and illustrations based on your personal experience. It is easy to fall back on being conceptual and abstract during question and answer sessions. The danger here is that your messages become vague, and your status drops.

Do: keep your vocal and physical energy up. AT ALL TIMES!

12:

CONCLUSION

I'll never forget my first day working at Bloomberg TV. I'd arrived from UBS as a political analyst, and while I'd often spoken as a 'talking head' on various political and economic matters, I'd never had to put my own material and graphs together and think through what a three-minute appearance on TV would actually be like.

At Bloomberg I was given a glass box, roughly the size of a dinner table for six, which had a camera and a microphone attached to it. I carefully prepared the graphs I was going to use to illustrate the dollar's move after a decision by the Federal Reserve Bank to raise interest rates. I made careful notes as to what I wanted to say and waited for the anchor to toss to me. And then it came. Mark Barton, the anchor, said, 'For reaction on that Federal Reserve rate hike, let's go over to Edie in the studio ' – and I was off!

About twenty seconds into my performance, I noticed on the TV screen that I was no longer on air. Rather, the anchor was smiling and reading a story about gold prices. I began to hear a rumble of laughter from outside my studio which echoed louder as my producer opened the studio, wiping tears out of his eyes. 'That was the funniest thing I've ever seen. You stepped too far away from the camera and your mic went sailing off – I think it ricocheted back and hit the lens!'

Not a great start to my career as a TV presenter. It's perhaps no surprise to hear that I borrowed a roll of electrical tape and blocked out my space on the floor immediately afterwards, cheeks still burning from the experience.

A week later, my producer came back into the studio and said, 'You're doing fine, but if you use the words "going forward" again, I think I'm going to pull my ears off.' Of course, the next few times I was on air I think I said 'going forward' about a hundred times because I was so rattled and worried about it. It took me over a week to get rid of the verbal habit.

I often get asked, 'Aren't some people just natural speakers?' As you can see, I had a lot to learn when I went on air. I had a background in covering and speaking about how politics affected the markets, but none of the 'natural' ability to appear on TV. I worked hard at it. I watched my hits, tried to improve on the many mistakes I made and got training.

I think saying some people are 'natural speakers' is a little like saying that Roger Federer is a natural tennis player. Of course he is brilliant and sporty. But he trains really hard – before tournaments he'll train over three hours a day in the sweltering heat of Dubai.* He takes it seriously, he works at his volleys, serves and returns and never rests on his laurels.

I do think some people are great speakers, just as there are great actors, tennis players or pianists. I also know they work hard at it. You can always be better. Steve Jobs, the late CEO of Apple, was renowned for working hard on his speeches. According to his biographers he 'rehearsed endlessly and fastidiously'.† Ahead of MacWorld keynote

---

* See http://straightsets.blogs.nytimes.com/2011/01/19/training-with-federer-in-dubai/?_r=0.
† Brent Schlender and Rick Tetzeli, *Becoming Steve Jobs*, 2015.

speeches he reviewed scripts, rehearsed and rehearsed again. His presentations looked effortless because he put an enormous amount of effort into them ahead of time.

Jobs' 2005 Stanford commencement address is a highly quotable speech, full of personal anecdotes from his own life. He wrote it himself, and walked around the house for days practising it. As his biographers Schlender and Tetzeli tell it, 'The kids watching their dad spring past them in the same kind of trance he'd sometimes enter in the days before Mac-World. Several times he read it to the whole family dinner.' On the day of the speech he was nervous. 'I'd almost never seen him more nervous,' his wife Laurene said.[*]

So: great speakers are nervous before big events that matter. Great speakers rehearse – and rehearse again. And then, when they appear, they look natural. They make it look easy, authentic and animated. And when they speak they have impact, because they've found ways to connect with their audience. They can't be ignored.

So take a breath, take the leap – and let me know how it goes!

---

[*] Ibid.

Authors' Note

Edie Lush wrote chapters
1, 2, 3, 4, 5, 7, 8, 10 and 12.

Charlotte McDougall wrote chapters
2, 6, 9 and 11.

Acknowledgements

Thanks to the following people for speaking to us and/or for granting us permission to use their words in this book:

Olivier Oullier
Alex (Sandy) Pentland
Laura Copeland
Marcus Geduld
Richard Harris
Matthew Barzun
Lucy Kellaway
Julia Streets
Uri Hasson
Paul J. Zak
Brian Massey
Michael Hayman
Jason Warner
William Poundstone
Sebastian Kernbach
Octavius Black
Ron Finley
Alan Siedel
Brent Schlender and Rick Tetzeli
TED
Sierra DeMulder
Joe Randazzo
Hamish Thompson
Lucian Tarnowski

Thanks to Alice Macdonald for the brilliant illustrations.

Index

acronyms 97, 107
Ambadi, Nalini 35–6, 35n
analogies 49–50, 52, 63, 134
anchoring 120–1, 128
anecdotes 48–9, 92, 99, 116, 133–4, 142
Arab Spring 42–3
audience:
    brain and reaction of 69–71, 72
    'energy vampires' and 10–11
    hooking the 41, 57, 122–4, 128
    storytelling and 67–71, 72
    tailoring speech for 96–7

Barzun, Matthew 58
behavioural questions 81–3, 82n, 85
Bernstein, Leonard: 'The Unanswered Question' 122
big speech see speech, big
Birdwhistell, Ray 8, 8n, 79n
Black, Octavius 123–4, 124n
Bloomberg 52, 97, 140
body:
    images and 108–13
    nerves and see nerves
    physical preparation and 74–6
body language:
    case study 91
    hands and 20–3
    importance to communication of 7–9, 8n, 39
    posture and 15–19
Bouazizi, Mohamed 42–3

brain:
    audience reception and areas of 69–71, 72
    empathy and 68, 72
    images and 55, 108–13
    mirroring and 13–14, 38, 119
    neural coupling 65–6, 72
    posture and 16, 39
    stories and 55, 65–6, 68, 69–71, 72
brainteaser questions 83–4
breathing:
    mindful 74–5
    nerves and 125
    running out of breath 24
Broca's area 69–71

case studies:
    big speech 114–19
    job interview 89–93
    pitching for business 129–39
channel energy, how to 38–9
Conkling, Rockwell 44
connective words 32, 33–4
Cook, Tim 60
Copeland, Laura 50, 50n
cortisol 16, 17, 21, 39, 68
Cuddy, Amy 15, 15n, 16, 21
CV 77, 85–6, 87, 130

Dale, Edgar 109, 109n
Darwin, Charles 15
DeMulder, Sierra 51
descriptions, using 43, 54–6, 63

dynamic energy 4, 6–40, 115, 128
  channelling energy 38–9
  energy levels 14–15
  feeling powerful and lack of 15–16
  look and sound of 14–15
  message, landing 9–14
  perception of those lacking 15
  physical energy and 17–24, 37–8
  vocal energy and 23–40

emotion:
  emphasis and 25, 26
  as a hook 57, 122
  stories and 56, 57, 63, 67–8, 71, 72
emphasis 25–7, 39, 127
endings, strong 125–8
  call to action and 126, 128
  energy techniques and 127
  finish 127–8
  hope, inspiring audience with 126
  message, bringing home your 127
  personal story, using 125, 128
  props, using 126
  quotations, using 125, 126, 128
  slides, using 126
  soundbites, using 126
  surprising fact, using 127
  three words that underscore your
    message, using 126–7
energy, dynamic see dynamic energy
'energy vampires' 11–13
examples, using 63, 87, 99–100, 116,
  118, 119, 133–4, 139
expansiveness, power signaling
  and 15–16
eye contact 37–8, 86, 87, 101, 117,
  128

facts and emotions, stories and 56, 63
fear of public speaking 1
filming speech 98, 103
finish 127–8 see also endings, strong
Finley, Ron 126, 126n
font choice, slide 103–5, 107

Geduld, Marcus 51, 51n
Giles, Nick 102
Gladwell, Malcolm: Blink 121, 121n
gravitas 31, 122

hands, use of 20–3
Hasson, Uri 65, 66, 66n
Hayman, Michael 77n, 102
hook, audience and 41, 57, 122–4,
  128
Horn, Robert 110, 111, 111n

'I' not 'we', use 43–6, 62, 82, 87
'idea porn' 71
infographic 110
interview, preparing for an 73–88
  case study 89–93
  how you say it 86–7
  physical preparation 74–6
  positive energy 86
  questions, asking your own 85
  questions, basic opening 80–1
  questions, behavioural 81–3
  questions, brainteaser 83–4
  questions, CV and 85–6
  questions, interviewer and 86
  questions, listening to 80
  verbal preparation 76–9
  what you say 87–8

jargon:
  audience and 96, 97, 106–7, 115,
    127n
  brain and 71, 72
  case studies and 115, 132
  effects of 58–62, 61n, 63
Jobs, Steve 126, 141–2, 141n
journey, stories as 46–7, 62, 67–8

Kellaway, Lucy 59, 60n
kinesics 8, 8n, 79n

language, using plain 63 see also body
  language and jargon

Lawson, Dominic 99–100
lectern 19, 118

Massey, Brian 69–71, 100, 100n
Mehrabian, Dr Albert 7–8, 7n
message:
    ending speeches and 127
    landing our 9–10
    slides and 103
    storytelling and 57–8, 64
metaphors 49, 50, 50n, 51n, 134
microphone 19, 27, 119
mindfulness 74–5, 98
mini-stories 48–9
mirroring 12–13, 14, 38, 119
monotone voice 6, 8, 23, 25, 27, 32,
    36, 119

name-checking 117–18
nerves 4, 10, 37, 70, 120, 124–5, 128,
    136
neural coupling 65–6, 66n, 72
neuro-linguistic programming 124
non-verbal behaviour 7–9
nosism (practice of using 'we' when we
    mean 'I') 45

opening questions 80–1, 85
Oullier, Professor Olivier 13, 13n, 38,
    102, 108, 122–3
overview map 110

pauses 27–38, 40, 77
    benefits of 29–31
    control during 32–7
    ending a speech and 127
    eye contact and 37–8
    fears about 31–2
    how it helps 39–40
    importance of 27–9
    nerves and 125
    Q&As and 137
    starting a speech and 121–2, 128
    two rules for 27

Pease, Allen and Barbara 8–9, 8n
Pentland, Alex (Sandy) 36, 36n
physical energy 17–40, 115, 136, 137,
    139
    body language and see body
        language
    channelling 36–7
    eye contact and 37–8
    hands and 20–3
    pauses and see pauses
    posture and 17–19
    smiling and 38
    vocal energy 23–40 see also vocal
        energy
physical preparation 74–6
pictures:
    likeability and 111–12
    meeting times and 110–11
    recall and 109–10
    slides and 105–6
    storytelling and 54–5, 62–3
    see also visuals
Pinter, Harold 31, 50
pitching for business 36, 59, 74,
    129–39
positive energy 22, 86
posture 15–19, 91
    sitting down 17–18
    standing up 18–19
Poundstone, William: How Would You
        Move Mount Fuji? 84, 84n
power poses 16, 21, 74–6
preparation:
    physical 74–6
    speech 117
    verbal 76–9
props 98–100, 117, 126, 128

Qahtani, Mohammed 99
questions, interview 80–6
    ask some yourself 85
    behavioural 81–3
    brainteaser 83–4
    CV and 85–6

questions, interview (*cont.*)
  interviewer and 86
  listening to 80
  opening 80–1
questions and answers (Q&As) 132, 136–9
Quora 50, 50*n*, 51, 51*n*
quotations, using 125, 126, 128

Randazzo, Joe 52
rapid cognition 121
rushing 24, 26, 137

SARI (Situation, Action, Result, Interesting Feature) 82–3
science, stories and 65–72
Seinfeld, Jerry 1
Siegel, Alan 126–7, 127*n*
Silbert, Lauren 65
similes 49, 51–2, 51*n*
slides 92, 101–6, 126
  colours on 106, 107
  cutting 118, 134
  endings and 126, 127
  font choice 103–4
  font size 104–5, 107
  one key message per 103, 107, 113
  overusing 118
  picture 105–6
  pitches and 134
  relying on to prompt you 118–19
  talking to 118
smiling 13–14, 38, 39, 87, 124, 125, 128
social coordination dynamics 13, 13*n*
speech, the big 94–107
  case study 114–19
  dos and don'ts 117–19
  filming of 98
  jargon or acronyms 97
  props 98–100
  questions to keep in mind 96
  slides 101–6
  stick to allotted time 106

tailoring for audience 96–7
  visuals/images 108–12
start strong, how to 120–5
  anchoring and 120–1
  hooking the audience 122–4
  nerves 124–5
  pausing and 121–2
  rapid cognition 121
Stephens, Greg 65
Stone, Rob 59–60
story, telling the 41–64
  analogies/similes/metaphors and 49–52
  characters, using 43, 53–6, 63, 68
  descriptions, using 54–6
  emotion as a hook, using 57
  facts and emotions and 56, 63
  'I' not 'we', using 43–6, 62
  jargon and 58–62
  journey, nature of 46–7
  language and 63
  message and 57–8, 64
  mini-stories and anecdotes and 48–9
  pictures/images/people and 62–3
  science and 65–72
Streets, Julia: *The Lingua Franca of the Corporate Banker* 61, 61*n*
surprising fact, finish with a 127
swallowing words 23
Swift, Taylor 86, 86*n*

Talmage, Thomas De Witt 45, 45*n*
Tarnowski, Lucian 124
TED talk 2, 94–5, 98, 104, 107, 120, 126–7
testosterone 16, 21, 39
Thompson, Hamish 61
time, allotted 106
tone of voice 6, 7, 8, 23, 25, 27, 32, 35–6, 119
transmit mode 19, 27, 29, 134
Twain, Mark 57

unconscious movements 118
Unique Selling Point (USP) 129
up an octave (vocal technique) 32–4,
       38
'upspeak' (ending the sentence
       sounding like a question) 24
'Use of Visualization in the
       Communication of Business
       Strategies: An Experimental
       Evaluation' (Kernbach, Eppler
       and Bresciani) 111–12, 112n

Venerable Bede, The 51
verbal preparation 76–9 see also vocal
       energy
visuals/images 108–13
   body and 108–13
   likeability and 111–12
   meeting times and 110–11
   recall and 109–10
   slides and see slides
   storytelling and 55, 63, 70
vocal energy/voice 23–40, 115, 119,
       136
   emphasis and 25–7

eye contact and 37–8
how it helps 39
ingredients of 24–40
microphones and 27
pause and 27 37
quiet voice 23, 115
running out of breath and 24
rushing and 24
smiling and 38
swallowing words and 23
tone of voice 6, 7, 8, 23, 25, 27, 32,
       35–6, 119
'upspeak' and 24
volume and 23–5, 26, 38, 87, 127

Warner, Jason 82
Wernicke's area 70, 71
Williams, Roy H. 69, 69n
Wizard Academy Institute 69
Worthington, Andrew 92

Zak, Paul J. 67–8, 68n
Zimmer, Ben 43–4, 44n
zoning out 6, 12, 23, 33